AWS Migration Hub User Guide

A catalogue record for this book is available from the Hong Kong Public Libraries.

Published in Hong Kong by Samurai Media Limited.

Email: info@samuraimedia.org

ISBN 9789888407736

Contents

What Is AWS Migration Hub?

AWS Migration Hub provides a single place to discover your existing servers, plan migrations, and track the status of each application migration. The AWS Migration Hub provides visibility into your application portfolio and streamlines planning and tracking. You can see the status of the servers and databases that make up each of the applications you are migrating regardless of which migration tool you are using.

AWS Migration Hub gives you the choice to start migrating right away and group servers while migration is underway, or to first discover servers and then group them into applications. Either way, you can migrate each server in an application and track progress from each tool in the AWS Migration Hub. It supports migration status updates from AWS Database Migration Service, AWS Server Migration Service, ATADATA ATAmotion, CloudEndure Live Migration, and Racemi DynaCenter.

For more information, open the AWS Migration Hub console at https://console.aws.amazon.com/migrationhub/, and in the navigation pane under **Migrate**, choose **Tools**. *Note that you must first have an AWS account and credentials to access the Migration Hub console - see* Setting Up.

Are You a First-Time User of AWS Migration Hub?

If you are a first-time user of AWS Migration Hub, we recommend that you read the following sections in order:

For a guide through the steps of migration, see the following topics:

- Getting Started
- Walkthroughs

If you want to learn about sending status to or querying status from AWS Migration Hub using the AWS SDK or AWS CLI, see:

- AWS Migration Hub API

Also, if you have a tool that you want to integrate with AWS Migration Hub, contact us by choosing **Feedback** in the lower left-hand corner of the footer in the AWS Migration Hub console. For all support issues, contact us here.

Setting Up

Before you use AWS Migration Hub for the first time, if you have not done so, complete the following tasks:

1. Sign Up for AWS
2. Create an IAM User

Sign Up for AWS

When you sign up for Amazon Web Services (AWS), you are charged only for the services that you use. If you already have an AWS account, you can skip this step.

If you have an AWS account already, skip to the next task. If you don't have an AWS account, use the following procedure to create one.

To create an AWS account

1. Open https://aws.amazon.com/, and then choose **Create an AWS Account. Note**
   This might be unavailable in your browser if you previously signed into the AWS Management Console. In that case, choose **Sign in to a different account**, and then choose **Create a new AWS account**.

2. Follow the online instructions.

   Part of the sign-up procedure involves receiving a phone call and entering a PIN using the phone keypad.

Note your AWS account number, because you'll need it for the next task.

Create an IAM User

Services in AWS, such as AWS Migration Hub, require that you provide credentials when you access them, so that the service can determine whether you have permissions to access its resources. AWS recommends that you do not use the root credentials of your AWS account to make requests. Instead, create an IAM user, and grant that user full access. We refer to these users as administrator users. You can use the administrator user credentials, instead of root credentials of your account, to interact with AWS and perform tasks, such as create a bucket, create users, and grant them permissions. For more information, see Root Account Credentials vs. IAM User Credentials in the *AWS General Reference* and IAM Best Practices in the *IAM User Guide*.

If you signed up for AWS but have not created an IAM user for yourself, you can create one using the IAM console.

To create an IAM user for yourself and add the user to an Administrators group

1. Use your AWS account email address and password to sign in as the *AWS account root user* to the IAM console at https://console.aws.amazon.com/iam/. **Note**
   We strongly recommend that you adhere to the best practice of using the **Administrator** user below and securely lock away the root user credentials. Sign in as the root user only to perform a few account and service management tasks.

2. In the navigation pane of the console, choose **Users**, and then choose **Add user**.

3. For **User name**, type ** Administrator**.

4. Select the check box next to **AWS Management Console access**, select **Custom password**, and then type the new user's password in the text box. You can optionally select **Require password reset** to force the user to select a new password the next time the user signs in.

5. Choose **Next: Permissions**.

6. On the **Set permissions for user** page, choose **Add user to group**.

7. Choose **Create group**.

8. In the **Create group** dialog box, type ** Administrators**.

9. For **Filter**, choose **Job function**.

10. In the policy list, select the check box for ** AdministratorAccess**. Then choose **Create group**.

11. Back in the list of groups, select the check box for your new group. Choose **Refresh** if necessary to see the group in the list.

12. Choose **Next: Review** to see the list of group memberships to be added to the new user. When you are ready to proceed, choose **Create user**.

You can use this same process to create more groups and users, and to give your users access to your AWS account resources. To learn about using policies to restrict users' permissions to specific AWS resources, go to Access Management and Example Policies.

To sign in as this new IAM user, sign out of the AWS Management Console, and then use the following URL, where *your_aws_account_id* is your AWS account number without the hyphens (for example, if your AWS account number is 1234-5678-9012, your AWS account ID is 123456789012):

```
1 https://your_aws_account_id.signin.aws.amazon.com/console/
```

Enter the IAM user name and password that you just created. When you're signed in, the navigation bar displays *your_user_name***@***your_aws_account_id*.

If you don't want the URL for your sign-in page to contain your AWS account ID, you can create an account alias. From the IAM dashboard, click **Create Account Alias** and enter an alias, such as your company name. To sign in after you create an account alias, use the following URL:

```
1 https://your_account_alias.signin.aws.amazon.com/console/
```

To verify the sign-in link for IAM users for your account, open the IAM console and check under **AWS Account Alias** on the dashboard.

Getting Started with AWS Migration Hub

In this section, you can find information about how to get started with AWS Migration Hub. Included are steps to introduce you to the initial console screens that Migration Hub presents to a new user.

- Assumptions
- Accessing AWS Migration Hub
- Two Ways to Get Started
- Perform Discovery and Then Migrate
- Migrate Without Performing Discovery

Note
If you are a developer or are interested in sending migration status from either a migration tool, script, or custom code, see AWS Migration Hub API.

Assumptions

For these exercises, the following is assumed:

- You have signed up for AWS. For more information, see Setting Up

- Migration Hub monitors the status of your migrations in all AWS regions, provided your migration tools are available in that region.

- The migration tools that integrate with Migration Hub send migration status to Migration Hub in us-west-2 where the status is aggregated and visible in a single location.

- The migration tools do not send status unless you have authorized (that is, connected) them.

- For a list of AWS regions where you can use Migration Hub, see the Amazon Web Services General Reference.

Accessing AWS Migration Hub

You can use AWS Migration Hub to track the status of application migrations. The Getting Started section and various other sections of this guide use the AWS Migration Hub console to illustrate migration functionality. You can find AWS Migration Hub at AWS Migration Hub.

Additionally, you can use the AWS Migration Hub API to track the status of your migrations from other tools or to send custom migration status to the AWS Migration Hub. For more information about the API, see AWS Migration Hub API.

You can also use the AWS SDKs to develop applications that interact with Migration Hub. The AWS SDKs for Java, .NET, and PHP wrap the underlying Migration Hub API to simplify your programming tasks. For information about downloading the SDK libraries, see Sample Code Libraries.

Two Ways to Get Started

If you want to discover detailed information about your servers using AWS discovery tools before migrating, see Perform Discovery and Then Migrate to guide you through the discovery process.

If you want to start migrating immediately without using AWS discovery tools, see Migrate Without Performing Discovery to guide you through starting to migrate and tracking the status in Migration Hub. You can also perform discovery at a later time if you want to gather server details.

If this is the first time you are using Migration Hub or you have not sent any data to Migration Hub yet, you will see the new user screen where you will be given the option to choose one of the two migration workflows.

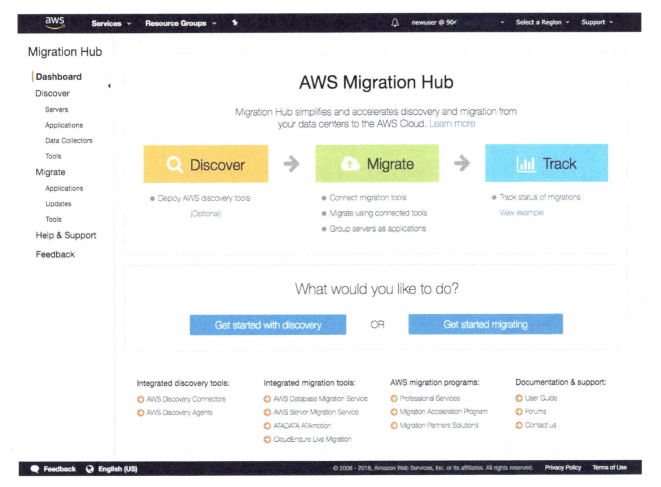

To begin your migration, choose either **Get started with discovery** or **Get started migrating** and then proceed to the respective workflow listed in the topics below.

Topics

- Option 1: Perform Discovery and Then Migrate
- Option 2: Migrate Without Performing Discovery

Perform Discovery and Then Migrate

Discovering your servers first is an optional starting point for migrations by gathering detailed server information and then grouping the discovered servers into applications to be migrated and tracked.

Use this section to guide you through the initial console screens that Migration Hub presents to the first-time user to view, compare, and download AWS discovery tools. *If you are not sure about the differences between the two AWS discovery tools, Discovery Connectors and Discovery Agents, see the AWS discovery tools comparison chart.*

Once you get past the new user screens, this section will reference the AWS Migration Hub Walkthroughs for remaining steps.

1. If you chose **Get started with discovery** in the new user screen, the **Perform Discovery and Then Migrate** screen is displayed. Choose **View AWS discovery tools**.

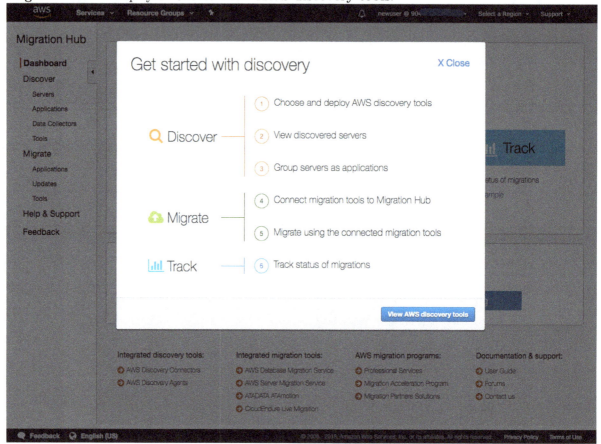

2. This takes you to the **Discovery Tools** page where you can download AWS discovery tools.

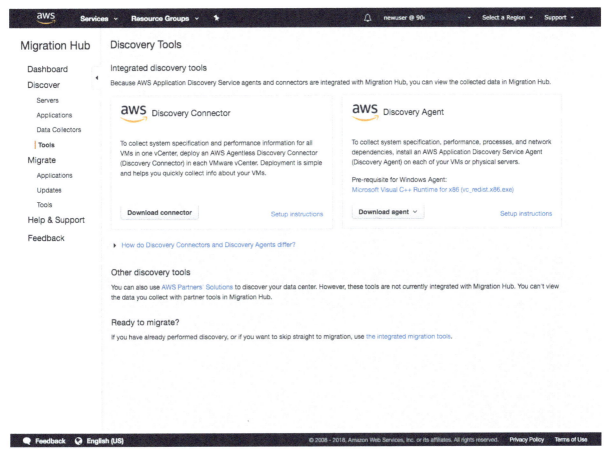

3. To proceed with next steps, see Phase 1: Discover of the Option 1: Perform Discovery and Then Migrate walkthrough.

Migrate Without Performing Discovery

Directly migrating servers is efficient because your servers are already migrating while you simultaneously group them into applications.

Use this section to guide you through the initial console screens that Migration Hub presents to the first-time user to view, compare, and connect AWS migration tools to Migration Hub. It is important to understand that connecting an AWS migration tool to Migration Hub is how you authorize that tool to communicate migration status to Migration Hub. Without this authorization, Migration Hub will not track your migration. *If you want to learn more about integrated migration tools, including AWS and partner tools, go to the **Migration Tools** page in Migration Hub (Migrate -> Tools) and follow the link to the documentation or to AWS Marketplce.*

Once you get past the new user screens, this section will reference the AWS Migration Hub Walkthroughs for remaining steps.

1. If you chose **Get started migrating** in the new user screen, the **Migrate Without Performing Discovery** screen is displayed. Choose **Connect migration tools**.

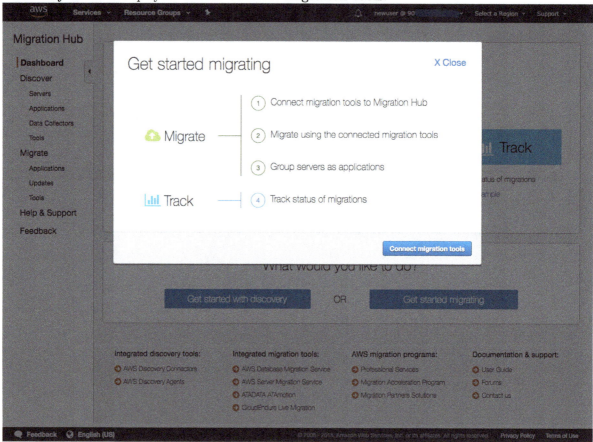

2. This takes you to the following screen where you can choose and authorize AWS migration tools or integrated partners' tools.

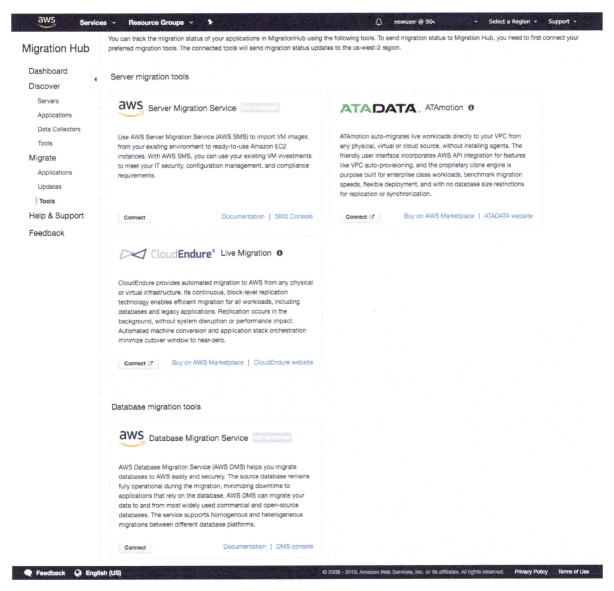

3. To proceed with next steps, see Phase 1: Migrate of the Option 2: Migrate Without Performing Discovery walkthrough.

AWS Migration Hub Walkthroughs

Use these walkthroughs to guide you through either of the two workflows of starting your migration:

- Discovery of servers' detail and then migration.
- Directly with migration without performing discovery.
- Option 1: Perform Discovery and Then Migrate
- Option 2: Migrate Without Performing Discovery

Option 1: Perform Discovery and Then Migrate

Discover

Here you will be guided through the workflow of starting your migration by first discovering your existing infrastructure using AWS discovery tools. You can download and deploy discovery connectors and/or discovery agents to discover your existing infrastructure. When one of these is deployed, you start data collection from the Migration Hub console.

Migration Hub's discovery process collects data about your existing environment using AWS discovery tools such as the AWS Agentless Discovery Connector and the AWS Application Discovery Agent. These discovery tools store their collected data in the Application Discovery Service's repository providing details about each server and the processes running on them. Application Discovery Service is another AWS service that is integrated with Migration Hub so that you can view your discovery data inside Migration Hub.

When you have discovered your servers and their respective data has been collected into the repository, you can view details about any server by choosing the server ID on the Servers page. Choosing a server ID brings you to a server detail page.

You can logically define and group all the discovered servers that comprise the applications you want to migrate.

Migrate

Migration happens outside Migration Hub and uses the supported migration tools. These tools include both AWS migration tools and integrated partners' migration tools. You can also group more servers into either an existing or a new application at a later time.

Track

Migration Hub helps you monitor the status of your migrations in all AWS regions, provided your migration tools are available in that region. The migration tools that integrate with the Migration Hub (e.g., SMS, DMS) send migration status to the Migration Hub in us-west-2. There, the status is aggregated and visible in a single location. These tools will not send status unless they have been authorized (that is, connected) by customers

These tools will not send status unless they have been connected (authorized).

The steps you will be doing in this walkthrough follow the outline of the **Perform Discovery and Then Migrate** workflow:

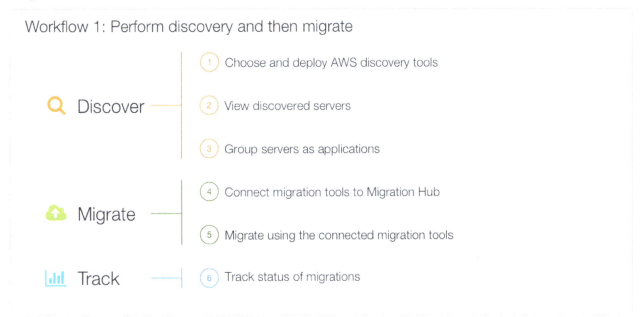

The following topics guide you through the three major steps of a discovery based migration workflow:

- Phase 1: Discover
- Phase 2: Migrate
- Phase 3: Track

Phase 1: Discover

The discovery phase has the following steps:

- Choose and Deploy AWS Discovery Tools.
- View Discovered Servers.
- Group Servers as Applications.
- Discover Step 1: Choose and Deploy AWS Discovery Tools
- Discover Step 2: View Discovered Servers
- Discover Step 3: Group Servers as Applications

Discover Step 1: Choose and Deploy AWS Discovery Tools

If you landed here from Step 3 of Perform Discovery and Then Migrate, or if you already have AWS discovery tools implemented and would like to deploy more, the following steps will show you how to deploy either an AWS Agentless Discovery Connector or an AWS Application Discovery Agent.

To help you decide whether to choose a Discovery Connector or a Discovery Agent, the following comparison chart is provided.

	Discovery Connector	Discovery Agent
Supported server types		
Virtual machine	✓	✓
Physical server		✓
Deployment		
Per server		✓
Per vCenter	✓	
Collected data		
Tech specs	✓	✓
Basic performance	✓	✓
Running processes		✓ (Export only)
Network dependencies		✓ (Export only)
Supported OS	Any OS running in **VMware vCenter** (V5.5 and V6.0)	**Linux** Amazon Linux 2012.03, 2015.03 Ubuntu 12.04, 14.04, 16.04 Red Hat Enterprise Linux 5.11, 6.9, 7.3 CentOS 5.11, 6.9, 7.3 SUSE 11 SP4, 12 SP2 **Windows** Windows Server 2003 R2 SP2 Windows Server 2008 R1 SP2, 2008 R2 SP1 Windows Server 2012 R1, 2012 R2 Windows Server 2016
Downloads	OVA	Windows agent Linux agent

Discovery Using the AWS Agentless Discovery Connector

These steps walk you through the discovery process using an AWS Agentless Discovery Connector for collecting data about your on-premises resources.

The Discovery Connector is a VMWare appliance (OVA) and can only collect information about VMWare VMs.

You use a Discovery Connector because it lets you quickly assess your infrastructure using a tool that isn't specific to any operating system, without having to install anything on the servers themselves.

To discover resources using an agentless connector

1. If you are proceeding from Step 3 of Perform Discovery and Then Migrate, choose **Download connector**; else, in the navigation pane, under **Discover**, choose **Tools**, and then choose **Download connector**.

2. Deploy and configure the agentless connector by following the instructions specified in Setting up Agentless Discovery from the AWS Application Discovery Service User Guide.

22

3. After you have successfully installed the agentless connector, return to the **Data Collectors** page on the Migration Hub console and choose the refresh icon.

4. Select the check box of the connector(s) you want to start.

5. Choose **Start data collection**.

   1. To install additional connectors, repeat the above procedure.

Discovery Using the AWS Application Discovery Agent

These steps walk you through the discovery process using an AWS Application Discovery Agent for collecting data about your on-premises resources.

You can install Discovery Agents on both your VMs and physical servers to not only discover your on-premises servers, but also to capture technical specifications, system performance, network dependencies, and process information. Network dependency and process information is available, but only for export. Use the Application Discovery Service CLI to export the data and analyze it outside of the Migration Hub. For more information, see describe-export-tasks.

The benefit of using a Discovery Agent is that it provides more detailed information than using the agentless Discovery Connector. This information includes system performance and resource utilization. In contrast, the benefit of using a discovery connector is that it provides a more efficient and faster on-premises infrastructure assessment.

To discover resources using an agent

1. If you are proceeding from Step 3 of Perform Discovery and Then Migrate, choose **Download agent**, then in the dropdown, select either **Windows** or **Linux**; else, the **Download agent** button can be accessed by choosing **Tools** under **Discover** in the navigation pane.

2. Deploy and configure the agent by following the instructions specified in Setting up Agent Based Discovery from the AWS Application Discovery Service User Guide.

3. After you have successfully installed the agent, return to the **Data Collectors** page on the Migration Hub console and choose the refresh icon.

4. Select the check box of the agent(s) you want to start.

5. Choose **Start data collection**.

   1. To install additional agents, repeat the above procedure.

Discover Step 2: View Discovered Servers

These steps walk you through viewing your servers that have been discovered after you have deployed and started your AWS discovery tool.

To view discovered servers

1. In the navigation pane, choose **Servers**. The discovered servers will be present in the servers list on this page. If you wish to see server details, proceed through the remaining steps.

2. Choose the server ID listed in the **Server ID** column. Doing so displays a screen that describes the server you selected.

3. The server's detail screen displays system information and performance metrics and a button for you to export network dependencies and processes information.

23

Discover Step 3: Group Servers as Applications

These steps walk you through the process of grouping servers as applications. Because applications can have multiple servers, it can help simplify migration tracking to group them into a logical unit.

The following steps will show you how to select the server(s) you want to group for your application, how to create your application and name it, and how to add identifying tags.

Tip

You can import application groups in bulk using the AWS CLI for Application Discovery Service and calling `CreateApplication` API (see AWS Application Discovery Service API guide).

To group servers into a new or existing application

1. In the navigation pane, choose **Servers**.

2. In the severs list, select the check-box for each of the servers you wish to group into a new or existing application.

    1. You can also search and filter on any of the criteria specified in the headers of the server list. Click inside the search bar and choose an item from the dropdown, then choose an operator from the next dropdown, and then type in your criteria.

    2. Optionally, for each selected server, you can add a descriptive tag by choosing **Add tag**. Doing so shows a dialog box where you can type a value for **Key**, and optionally a value for **Value**.

3. Create your application, or add to an existing one, by choosing **Group as application**.

4. In the **Group as application** dialog box, select either **Group as a new application** or **Add to an existing application**.

    1. If you chose **Group as a new application**, type a name in the **Application name** field. Optionally, you can type a description for **Application description**.

    2. If you chose **Add to an existing application**, select the radio button next to the application name in the list box.

5. Choose **Save**. A green confirmation message is displayed at the top of the screen.

Next steps

Once you have completed the three steps of the Discover phase, proceed to

- Phase 2: Migrate

Phase 2: Migrate

The migrate phase has the following steps:

- Connect Migration Tools to Migration Hub.
- Migrate Using the Connected Migration Tools.
- Migrate Step 1: Connect Migration Tools to Migration Hub
- Migrate Step 2: Migrate Using the Connected Migration Tools

Migrate Step 1: Connect Migration Tools to Migration Hub

Migration happens outside Migration Hub using AWS migration tools or integrated partners' migration tools. You choose these tools through the Tools page in the Migrate section in Migration Hub.

The table following lists the supported tools.

Resource type	Migration tool name
Server	AWS Server Migration Service ATADATA ATAmotion CloudEndure Live Migration Racemi DynaCenter
Database	AWS Database Migration Service

The preceding tools communicate directly to Migration Hub giving an aggregated view of their migrated progress and status so they can be tracked through Migration Hub.

The following steps walk you through connecting (authorizing) your selected migration tool.

To connect (authorize) a migration tool

1. In the navigation pane under **Migrate**, choose **Tools**.

2. Decide upon which AWS migration tools or integrated partners' tools to migrate your application.

3. Choose **Connect** in the box to authorize the migration tool you selected to communicate with Migration Hub.

   1. AWS migration tools utilize a one-click authorization process which automatically adds the required permissions role once you choose **Connect**.

   2. Integrated partners' tools take you to their website when you choose **Connect** where you will be instructed on how to complete authorization.

Note
Note that if you are using API's or do not want to authorize through Migration Hub's console, you can learn about manual role creation in New User IAM Setup.

Migrate Step 2: Migrate Using the Connected Migration Tools

The following steps walk you through the migration of a previously defined application.

To migrate an application

1. In the navigation pane under **Migrate**, choose **Tools**.

2. If you connected (authorized) an AWS migration tool, choose the console link. If you connected (authorized) an integrated partner's tool, choose the website link.

3. When you have been linked to either the tool's console or website, follow the migration instructions for your selected migration tool as migration happens outside of Migration Hub.

4. When your application's migration has started, return to Migration Hub.

Next steps

Once you have completed the two steps of the Migrate phase, proceed to

- Phase 3: Track

Phase 3: Track

In the track phase, you track the status of migrations.

- Track Status of Migrations.
- Track Step 1: Track Status of Migrations

Track Step 1: Track Status of Migrations

To track an application's migration status

1. When your application's migration has started, return to Migration Hub and choose **Dashboard**.

2. In the top pane labeled **Most recently updated applications**, click inside the donut chart labeled with the name of your migrating application. This displays the application's detail screen.

    1. If you do not see all of your application's servers listed in the application's details page, it might be because you have not grouped those servers into this application yet. If you do not see the migration status of a server, automapping to discovered servers may have mapped to the wrong server and you need to manually edit the mapping. See Updates About My Migrations Don't Appear Inside an Application.

3. After verifying the in-progress migration status from the application's detail screen, you will want to change the application migration status from "Not started" to "In-progress". Choose **Change status** in the upper, right-hand corner.

4. Select the radio button next to **In-progress** in the dialog box.

5. Choose **Save**. A green confirmation message appears at the top of the screen, and the status label changes to **In-progress**.

6. Continue to monitor the application's migration status from the data presented in the application's detail screen by refreshing your browser or by clicking the refresh button preceding the server table on the application details page.

7. When the data in the application's detail screen indicates migration has completed, and you've performed testing and verification, you will want to change the status from "In-progress" to "Completed". Choose **Change status** in the top right corner of the page.

8. Select the radio button next to **Completed** in the pop-up list box.

9. Choose **Save**. A green confirmation message appears at the top of the screen, and the status label changes to **Completed**.

Option 2: Migrate Without Performing Discovery

Following, you can find the workflow of starting your migration by directly using integrated AWS migration tools or integrated partners' migration tools without performing discovery with AWS discovery tools. Migration happens outside Migration Hub using these integrated migration tools

Migrate
As you perform the migration, the servers you are migrating appear in the servers page in the discover section so that you can logically define and group all the servers that comprise the applications you are migrating. You can also group more servers into either an existing or a new application at a later time.

Track
With a migration underway, you can track its progress status as well as details for each server grouped to the application. This status is communicated to Migration Hub from the migration tool at key points during the migration.

The steps you will be doing in this walkthrough follow the outline of the **Migrate Without Performing Discovery**.

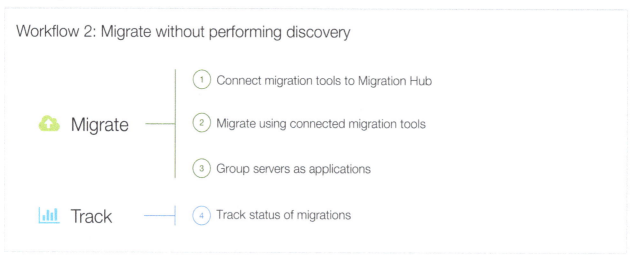

The following topics guide you through the three major steps of a direct to migration workflow.

- Phase 1: Migrate
- Phase 2: Track

Phase 1: Migrate

The migrate phase has the following steps:

- Connect Migration Tools to Migration Hub.
- Migrate Using the Connected Migration Tools.
- Group Servers as Applications.
- Migrate Step 1: Connect Migration Tools to Migration Hub
- Migrate Step 2: Migrate Using the Connected Migration Tools
- Migrate Step 3: Group Servers as Applications

Migrate Step 1: Connect Migration Tools to Migration Hub

If you landed here from Step 3 of Migrate Without Performing Discovery, the following steps will show you how to authorize a migration tool and begin migrating.

Migration happens outside Migration Hub using AWS migration tools or integrated partners' migration tools. You choose these tools through the Tools page in the Migrate section in Migration Hub.

The table following lists the supported tools.

Resource type	Migration tool name
Server	AWS Server Migration Service ATADATA ATAmotion CloudEndure Live Migration Racemi DynaCenter
Database	AWS Database Migration Service

The preceding tools communicate directly to Migration Hub giving an aggregated view of their migrated progress and status so they can be tracked through Migration Hub.

The following steps walk you through connecting (authorizing) your selected migration tool.

To connect (authorize) a migration tool

1. In the navigation pane under **Migrate**, choose **Tools**.

2. Decide upon which AWS migration tools or integrated partners' tools to migrate your application.

3. Choose **Connect** in the box to authorize the migration tool you selected to communicate with Migration Hub.

    1. AWS migration tools utilize a one-click authorization process which automatically adds the required permissions role once you choose **Connect**.

    2. Integrated partners' tools take you to their website when you choose **Connect** where you will be instructed on how to complete authorization.

Note
Note that if you are using API's or do not want to authorize through Migration Hub's console, you can learn about manual role creation in New User IAM Setup.

Migrate Step 2: Migrate Using the Connected Migration Tools

The following steps walk you through the migration of a previously defined application.

To migrate an application

1. In the navigation pane under **Migrate**, choose **Tools**.

2. If you connected (authorized) an AWS migration tool, choose the console link. If you connected (authorized) an integrated partner's tool, choose the website link.

3. When you have been linked to either the tool's console or website, follow the migration instructions for your selected migration tool as migration happens outside of Migration Hub.

4. When your application's migration has started, return to Migration Hub.

Migrate Step 3: Group Servers as Applications

These steps walk you through the process of grouping servers as applications when directly migrating with a migration tool without performing discovery first.

When the migration tool has started, you will see the servers listed in Migration Hub from the migration updates sent from the migration tool. You can select the servers and group them as applications. Keep in mind that the server information communicated to Migration Hub from the migration tool is not as detailed as what is collected from a discovery tool.

The following steps will show you how to select the server or servers you want to group for your application, how to create your application and name it, and how to add identifying tags.

To group servers into a new or existing application

1. In the navigation pane, select **Servers**.

2. In the severs list, select the checkbox for each of the servers you want to group into a new or existing application.

    1. You can also search and filter on any of the criteria specified in the headers of the server list. Click inside the search bar and choose an item from the dropdown, then choose an operator from the next dropdown, and then type in your criteria.

    2. Optionally, for each selected server, you can add a descriptive tag by choosing **Add tag**. A dialog box appears where you can type a value for **Key**, and optionally, a value for **Value**.

3. Create your application, or add to an existing one, by choosing **Group as application**.

4. In the **Group as application** dialog box, select either **Group as a new application** or **Add to an existing application**.

    1. If you chose **Group as a new application**, type a name for **Application name**. Optionally, you can type a description for **Application description**.

    2. If you chose **Add to an existing application**, select the radio button next to the application name in the list box.

5. Choose **Save**. A green confirmation message appears at the top of the screen.

Next steps

Once you have completed the three steps of the Migrate phase, proceed to

- Phase 2: Track

Phase 2: Track

In the track phase, you track the status of migrations.

- Track Status of Migrations.
- Track Step 1: Track Status of Migrations

Track Step 1: Track Status of Migrations

To track an application's migration status

1. Because you started your migration after you connected (authorized) your migration tool(s) and also grouped servers as applications in prior steps, your applications will already be present in Migration Hub's dashboard.

2. In the top pane labeled **Most recently updated applications**, click inside the donut chart labeled with the name of your migrating application. Doing this displays the application's detail screen.

   1. If you do not see all of your application's servers listed in the application's details page, it could be because you have not grouped those servers into this application yet. See Updates About My Migrations Don't Appear Inside an Application.

3. After verifying the in-progress migration status from the application's detail screen, you will want to change the application migration status from "Not started" to "In-progress". Choose **Change status** in the upper, right-hand corner.

4. Select the radio button next to **In-progress** in the dialog box.

5. Choose **Save**. A green confirmation message appears at the top of the screen, and the status label changes to **In-progress**.

6. Continue to monitor the application's migration status from the data presented in the application's detail screen by refreshing your browser or by clicking the refresh button preceding the server table on the application details page.

7. When the data in the application's detail screen indicates migration has completed, and you've performed testing and verification, change the status from "In-progress" to "Completed" by choosing **Change status** in the top right corner of the page.

8. Select the radio button next to **Completed** in the box.

9. Choose **Save**. A green confirmation message appears at the top of the screen, and the status label changes to **Completed**.

Doing More in Migration Hub

This section contains additional information to help enrich your migration experience by providing details on how to fully utilize the Migration Hub console discussed in the following topics:

- Tracking Migration Updates
- Tracking Metrics Using the Dashboards
- Navigating from the Dashboard and the Navigation Pane

Tracking Migration Updates

In order to better understand how Migration Hub helps you monitor progress of a migration, there are three concepts to understand in the Migration Hub:

- Applications
- Resources (for example, servers)
- Updates

Migration tools like AWS SMS, AWS DMS, and integrated partners' tools send updates to AWS Migration Hub. These updates include information about how a particular resource migration (for example, server or database) is progressing. One or more resources are grouped together to make an application. Each application has a dedicated page in Migration Hub where you can go to see the updates for all the resources in the application.

When Migration Hub receives an update, it is displayed on the updates page. There can be a delay of up to five minutes for the initial update to appear in the updates page.

Tracking When You Perform Discovery First and Then Migrate

If you started performing discovery using AWS discovery tools, the servers list will likely be populated before you start migrating. Migration Hub attempts to automatically map updates from migration tools to servers in the servers list. If it cannot find a match in the discovered servers list, then Migration Hub will add a server corresponding to the migration update to the servers list and automatically map the update to the server.

Sometimes, when using AWS discovery tools, the automatic mapping of migration updates to servers can be incorrect. You can see updates and their mappings on the **Updates** page and can correct the mapping by choosing **Edit**.

See Step 2.a in *To determine if a migration update must be manually mapped to a discovered server* procedures below. If you have to frequently correct mappings after performing discovery, please contact AWS Support.

To determine if a migration update must be manually mapped to a discovered server

1. In the navigation pane, under **Migrate**, select **Updates**.

2. Verify if the **Mapped servers** column is populated for every row of migration updates.

    1. If the **Mapped servers** column is populated for every row of migration updates, this means auto-mapping was supported by the migration tool and manual mapping is not required. *You can edit the server mapping by choosing **Edit** next to the server name.*

    2. If one or more rows of the **Mapped servers** columns is *not* populated and there is a **Map** button present in that row's **Action** column, this is an indication that manual mapping is required. Proceed to the next set of procedures.

Tracking When You Migrate Without Performing Discovery

If you did not perform discovery with an AWS discovery tool, then Migration Hub will add a server corresponding to the migration update to the servers list and automatically map the update to the server. You can group servers to applications and then start tracking the migration on the application's details page in the **Migrate** section of the console. See, Group Servers as Applications and Track Status of Migrations.

Troubleshooting and Manually Mapping Migration Updates

You can verify that the migration update is mapped to a server by viewing the update on the **Updates** page. If a server has not been mapped to a migration and you just started the migration task, see if it appears as mapped after waiting five minutes and refreshing the page.

If after an initial wait of five minutes the update is still not mapped to a server, then you can manually map the update to a server by selecting the **Map** button. For more information, see the following procedure, *To manually map a migration update to a discovered server.* For officially supported migration tools, you should not need to manually map migration updates. If this happens frequently, please contact AWS Support.

The following steps show you how to manually map a migration update to a discovered server that was not able to be automapped.

To manually map a migration update to a discovered server

1. In the navigation pane, under **Migrate**, select **Updates**.

2. For each migration update row that has a **Map** button present in the **Action** column, select the **Map** button.

3. In the **Map to discovered server** box, select the radio button of the server you want to map to the migration update.

4. Choose **Save**. A green confirmation message appears at the top of the screen.

5. Verify that the server name of the server you just mapped is now present in the **Mapped servers** column.

Tracking Metrics Using the Dashboards

Dashboards provide a way to quickly see status and progress summary data, and also help you navigate to more detailed data.

Main Dashboard

The main dashboard gathers data from the Discover and Migrate dashboards in a central location.

The main dashboard consists of four at-a-glance status and information panes as well as a consolidated list of links for quick access. These panes allow you to understand the summary status of most recently updated applications and also get quick access to any of them, to get an overview of applications in different states, and to track the migration progress over time.

To reach the main dashboard, choose **Dashboard** from the navigation pane.

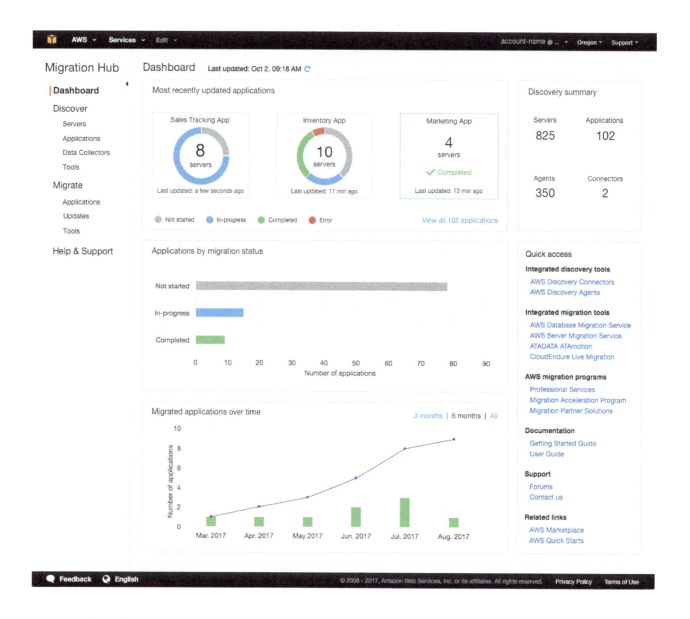

Navigating from the Dashboard and the Navigation Pane

After viewing dashboard data summaries, you might want to retrieve more detail without interrupting your workflow. You do this by navigating directly from the relevant status or information pane on the dashboard.

In the table following, you can find instructions on how to navigate from a dashboard to the information you want to see. You can also find instructions on how to get to this information by using the navigation pane.

To See	Do This	Which Is the Same As
All servers	From the total number of servers inside the Discovery summary box in the Main dashboard, choose **View all servers.**	[See the AWS documentation website for more details]

To See	Do This	Which Is the Same As
All agents	From the total number of agents in the Discovery summary box in the Main Dashboard, choose **View all agents**.	[See the AWS documentation website for more details]
All connectors	From the total number of connectors in the Discovery summary box in the Main dashboard, choose **View all connectors**.	[See the AWS documentation website for more details]
All applications	From either the Main dashboard or Migrate dashboard, in the Most recently updated applications pane, choose **View all applications** Or, from the Discover dashboard in the Servers & Applications pane, choose **View all applications**.	[See the AWS documentation website for more details]
Application details... [See the AWS documentation website for more details]	From either the Main dashboard or Migrate dashboard in the Most recently updated applications box, choose the application's status box.	[See the AWS documentation website for more details]
Server details... [See the AWS documentation website for more details]	From either the Main dashboard or Migrate dashboard, in the Most recently updated applications pane, choose the application. Then choose the server name in the Server ID column.	[See the AWS documentation website for more details]

Authentication and Access Control for AWS Migration Hub

Access to AWS Migration Hub requires credentials that AWS can use to authenticate your requests. Those credentials must have permissions to access AWS resources, such as an AWS Migration Hub ProgressUpdateStream or an Amazon EC2 instance. The following sections provide details on how you can use AWS Identity and Access Management (IAM) and Migration Hub to help secure your resources by controlling who can access them:

- Authentication
- Access Control

Authentication

You can access AWS as any of the following types of identities:

- **AWS account root user** – When you first create an AWS account, you begin with a single sign-in identity that has complete access to all AWS services and resources in the account. This identity is called the AWS account *root user* and is accessed by signing in with the email address and password that you used to create the account. We strongly recommend that you do not use the root user for your everyday tasks, even the administrative ones. Instead, adhere to the best practice of using the root user only to create your first IAM user. Then securely lock away the root user credentials and use them to perform only a few account and service management tasks.

- **IAM user** – An IAM user is an identity within your AWS account that has specific custom permissions (for example, permissions to create a function in AWS Migration Hub). You can use an IAM user name and password to sign in to secure AWS webpages like the AWS Management Console, AWS Discussion Forums, or the AWS Support Center.

  In addition to a user name and password, you can also generate access keys for each user. You can use these keys when you access AWS services programmatically, either through one of the several SDKs or by using the AWS Command Line Interface (CLI). The SDK and CLI tools use the access keys to cryptographically sign your request. If you don't use AWS tools, you must sign the request yourself. AWS Migration Hub supports *Signature Version 4*, a protocol for authenticating inbound API requests. For more information about authenticating requests, see Signature Version 4 Signing Process in the *AWS General Reference*.

- **IAM role** – An IAM role is an IAM identity that you can create in your account that has specific permissions. It is similar to an *IAM user*, but it is not associated with a specific person. An IAM role enables you to obtain temporary access keys that can be used to access AWS services and resources. IAM roles with temporary credentials are useful in the following situations:

  - **Federated user access** – Instead of creating an IAM user, you can use existing user identities from AWS Directory Service, your enterprise user directory, or a web identity provider. These are known as *federated users*. AWS assigns a role to a federated user when access is requested through an identity provider. For more information about federated users, see Federated Users and Roles in the *IAM User Guide*.

  - **AWS service access** – You can use an IAM role in your account to grant an AWS service permissions to access your account's resources. For example, you can create a role that allows Amazon Redshift to access an Amazon S3 bucket on your behalf and then load data from that bucket into an Amazon Redshift cluster. For more information, see Creating a Role to Delegate Permissions to an AWS Service in the *IAM User Guide*.

- **Applications running on Amazon EC2** – You can use an IAM role to manage temporary credentials for applications that are running on an EC2 instance and making AWS API requests. This is preferable to storing access keys within the EC2 instance. To assign an AWS role to an EC2 instance and make it available to all of its applications, you create an instance profile that is attached to the instance. An instance profile contains the role and enables programs that are running on the EC2 instance to get temporary credentials. For more information, see Using an IAM Role to Grant Permissions to Applications Running on Amazon EC2 Instances in the *IAM User Guide*.

Access Control

You can have valid credentials to authenticate your requests, but unless you have permissions you cannot create or access AWS Migration Hub resources. For example, you must have permissions to create a Migration Hub API type, `ProgressUpdateStream`, to use the AWS Application Discovery Service, and to use AWS migration tools.

The following sections describe how to manage permissions for AWS Migration Hub.

- AWS Migration Hub Roles and Policies
- AWS Migration Hub API Permissions: Actions and Resources Reference
- AWS Migration Hub Authentication and Access Control Explained

AWS Migration Hub Roles and Policies

Access to AWS Migration Hub requires credentials that AWS can use to authenticate your requests as well as have permissions to access AWS resources. The following sections demonstrate how the various permissions policies can be attached to IAM identities (that is, users, groups, and roles) and thereby grant permissions to perform actions on AWS Migration Hub resources.

The various types of permission polices referenced in this section have been explained in Using Identity-Based Policies (IAM Policies) for AWS Migration Hub. If you have not yet read that section, it is recommended that you do to gain a thorough understanding of the different types of polices before proceeding to use the policy templates in this section.

The policy templates have been organized in the following hierarchy as shown below. You can click on any policy to go directly to its template.

- New User IAM Setup
- Custom Policies for Migration Tools

New User IAM Setup

This section provides an overview of the four managed policies that can be used with AWS Migration Hub as well as instructions on how to setup access to either the Migration Hub console or its APIs for users or migration tools.

Required Managed Policies

The following AWS managed policies, which you can attach to users in your account, are specific to Migration Hub and are grouped by use case scenario:

- **AWSMigrationHubDiscoveryAccess** – (Included in the **migrationhub-discovery** role) – Grants permission to allow the Migration Hub service to call Application Discovery Service.

- **AWSMigrationHubFullAccess** – Grants access to the Migration Hub console and API/CLI for an user who's not an administrator.

- **AWSMigrationHubSMSAccess** – Grants permission for Migration Hub to receive notifications from the AWS Server Migration Service migration tool.

- **AWSMigrationHubDMSAccess** – Grants permission for Migration Hub to receive notifications from the AWS Database Migration Service migration tool.

If you want to grant Migration Hub rights to non-admin IAM users, then see Migration Hub Service API and Console Managed Access.

If you want to authorize (that is, connect) AWS migration tools, see AWS Server Migration Service (SMS) or AWS Database Migration Service (DMS).

Migration Hub Service API and Console Managed Access

An administrator can create users and grant them permission to access the Migration Hub console using managed policies.

1. Navigate to the IAM console.

2. Create a user.

3. Once the user is created, on the permissions tab select "Add Permissions".

4. Select "Attach existing policies directly".

5. Search for and attach the policy "AWSMigrationHubFullAccess".

migrationhub-discovery Role

To use Migration Hub, the `migrationhub-discovery` role (which contains the `AWSMigrationHubDiscoveryAccess` policy) must be added to your AWS account. It allows Migration Hub to access the Application Discovery Service on your behalf.

The AWS Migration Hub console creates the `migrationhub-discovery` role that is automatically attached to your AWS account when you use the Migration Hub console as an administrator. If you use the AWS Command Line Interface (AWS CLI) or the AWS Migration Hub API without also using the console, you need to manually add this role to your account.

1. Navigate to the IAM console Roles section.

2. Choose **Create new role**.

3. Select "Amazon EC2" from AWS Service Role.

4. Attach the "AWSApplicationDiscoveryServiceFullAccess" managed policy.

5. Name the role "migrationhub-discovery" *(required role name using exact case and spelling)*.

6. Access the new role and on the Trust Relationships tab, choose **Edit Trust Relationship**.

7. Add the trust policy below.

```
1  {
2    "Version": "2012-10-17",
3    "Statement": [
4      {
5        "Effect": "Allow",
6        "Principal": {
7          "Service": "migrationhub.amazonaws.com"
8        },
9        "Action": "sts:AssumeRole"
10     }
11   ]
12 }
```

Migration Tools (Managed Policies)

Roles and policies are needed for each migration tool in order for the Migration Hub to receive notifications from migration tools. These permissions allow AWS services like SMS and DMS to send updates to Migration Hub.

AWS Server Migration Service (SMS)

1. Navigate to the IAM console Roles section.

2. Choose **Create new role**.

3. Select "Amazon EC2" from AWS Service Role.

4. Attach the "AWSMigrationHubSMSAccess" managed policy.

5. Name the role "migrationhub-sms" *(required role name using exact case and spelling)*.

6. Access the new role, and on the Trust Relationships tab, choose **Edit Trust Relationship**.

7. Add the trust policy below.

```
1  {
2    "Version": "2012-10-17",
3    "Statement": [
4      {
5        "Effect": "Allow",
6        "Principal": {
7          "Service": [
8            "sms.amazonaws.com"
9          ]
10       },
11       "Action": "sts:AssumeRole"
12     }
13   ]
14 }
```

AWS Database Migration Service (DMS)

1. Navigate to the IAM console Roles section.

2. Choose **Create new role**.

3. Select "Amazon EC2" from AWS Service Role.

4. Attach the "AWSMigrationHubDMSAccess" managed policy.

5. Name the role "migrationhub-dms" *(required role name using exact case and spelling)*.

6. Access the new role, and on the Trust Relationships tab, choose **Edit Trust Relationship**.

7. Add the trust policy below.

```
{
  "Version": "2012-10-17",
  "Statement": [
    {
      "Effect": "Allow",
      "Principal": {
        "Service": [
          "dms.amazonaws.com"
        ]
      },
      "Action": "sts:AssumeRole"
    }
  ]
}
```

Custom Policies for Migration Tools

This is an example role for use by a integrated partner or developer when using the AWS Migration Hub API or CLI.

Integrated Partner Role Policy

```
1  {
2      "Version": "2012-10-17",
3      "Statement": [
4          {
5              "Action": [
6                  "mgh:CreateProgressUpdateStream"
7              ],
8              "Effect": "Allow",
9              "Resource": "arn:aws:mgh:us-west-2:account_num:progressUpdateStream/vendor_name"
10         },
11         {
12             "Action": [
13                 "mgh:AssociateCreatedArtifact",
14                 "mgh:DescribeMigrationTask",
15                 "mgh:DisassociateCreatedArtifact",
16                 "mgh:ImportMigrationTask",
17                 "mgh:ListCreatedArtifacts",
18                 "mgh:NotifyMigrationTaskState",
19                 "mgh:PutResourceAttributes",
20                 "mgh:NotifyApplicationState",
21                 "mgh:DescribeApplicationState",
22                 "mgh:AssociateDiscoveredResource",
23                 "mgh:DisassociateDiscoveredResource",
24                 "mgh:ListDiscoveredResources"
25             ],
26             "Effect": "Allow",
27             "Resource": "arn:aws:mgh:us-west-2:account_num:progressUpdateStream/vendor_name/*"
28         },
29         {
30             "Action": [
31                 "mgh:ListMigrationTasks"
32             ],
33             "Effect": "Allow",
34             "Resource": "*"
35         }
36     ]
37 }
```

Integrated Partner Policy Trust Policy

```
1  {
2      "Version": "2012-10-17",
3      "Statement": [
4          {
5              "Effect": "Allow",
6              "Principal": {
```

```
 7          "AWS": "arn:aws:iam::vendor_account_num:root"
 8        },
 9        "Action": "sts:AssumeRole"
10      }
11    ]
12  }
```

AWS Migration Hub API Permissions: Actions and Resources Reference

When you are setting up Access Control and writing a permissions policy that you can attach to an IAM identity (identity-based policies), you can use the following table as a reference. The table lists each Migration Hub API operation, the corresponding actions for which you can grant permissions to perform the action, and the AWS resource for which you can grant the permissions. You specify the actions in the policy's `Action` field, and you specify the resource value in the policy's `Resource` field.

Note

To specify an action, use the `mgh:` prefix followed by the API operation name (for example, `mgh: CreateProgressUpdateStream`).

If you see an expand arrow () in the upper-right corner of the table, you can open the table in a new window. To close the window, choose the close button (**X**) in the lower-right corner.

AWS Migration Hub API and Required Permissions for Actions

Migration Hub API Operations	Required Permissions (API Actions)	Resources
AssociateCreatedArtifact	mgh:AssociateCreatedArtifact	arn:aws:mgh:region:account-id:ProgressUpdateStreamName/resource-id or arn:aws:mgh:region:account-id:ProgressUpdateStreamName/resource-id/*
AssociateDiscoveredResource	mgh:AssociateDiscoveredResource	arn:aws:mgh:region:account-id:ProgressUpdateStreamName/resource-id or arn:aws:mgh:region:account-id:ProgressUpdateStreamName/resource-id/*
CreateProgressUpdateStream	mgh:CreateProgressUpdateStream	arn:aws:mgh:region:account-id:ProgressUpdateStreamName/resource-id
DeleteProgressUpdateStream	mgh:DeleteProgressUpdateStream	arn:aws:mgh:region:account-id:ProgressUpdateStreamName/resource-id
DescribeApplicationState	mgh:DescribeApplicationState	arn:aws:mgh:region:account-id:ProgressUpdateStreamName/resource-id or arn:aws:mgh:region:account-id:ProgressUpdateStreamName/resource-id/*

Migration Hub API Operations	Required Permissions (API Actions)	Resources
DescribeMigrationTask	mgh:DescribeMigrationTask	arn:aws:mgh:region:account-id:ProgressUpdateStreamName/resource-id or arn:aws:mgh:region:account-id:ProgressUpdateStreamName/resource-id/*
DisassociateCreatedArtifact	mgh:DisassociateCreatedArtifact	arn:aws:mgh:region:account-id:ProgressUpdateStreamName/resource-id or arn:aws:mgh:region:account-id:ProgressUpdateStreamName/resource-id/*
DisassociateDiscoveredResource	mgh:DisassociateDiscoveredResource	arn:aws:mgh:region:account-id:ProgressUpdateStreamName/resource-id or arn:aws:mgh:region:account-id:ProgressUpdateStreamName/resource-id/*
ImportMigrationTask	mgh:ImportMigrationTask	arn:aws:mgh:region:account-id:ProgressUpdateStreamName/resource-id or arn:aws:mgh:region:account-id:ProgressUpdateStreamName/resource-id/*
ListCreatedArtifacts	mgh:ListCreatedArtifacts	arn:aws:mgh:region:account-id:ProgressUpdateStreamName/resource-id or arn:aws:mgh:region:account-id:ProgressUpdateStreamName/resource-id/*
ListDiscoveredResources	mgh:ListDiscoveredResources	arn:aws:mgh:region:account-id:ProgressUpdateStreamName/resource-id or arn:aws:mgh:region:account-id:ProgressUpdateStreamName/resource-id/*
ListMigrationTasks	mgh:ListMigrationTasks	*
ListProgressUpdateStreams	mgh:ListProgressUpdateStreams	*
NotifyApplicationState	mgh:NotifyApplicationState	arn:aws:mgh:region:account-id:ProgressUpdateStreamName/resource-id or arn:aws:mgh:region:account-id:ProgressUpdateStreamName/resource-id/*
NotifyMigrationTaskState	mgh:NotifyMigrationTaskState	arn:aws:mgh:region:account-id:ProgressUpdateStreamName/resource-id or arn:aws:mgh:region:account-id:ProgressUpdateStreamName/resource-id/*

Migration Hub API Operations	Required Permissions (API Actions)	Resources
PutResourceAttributes	mgh:PutResourceAttributes	arn:aws:mgh:region:account-id:ProgressUpdateStreamName/resource-id or arn:aws:mgh:region:account-id:ProgressUpdateStreamName/resource-id/*

Related Topics

- Access Control

AWS Migration Hub Authentication and Access Control Explained

Overview of Managing Access Permissions to Your AWS Migration Hub Resources

Every AWS resource is owned by an AWS account, and permissions to create or access a resource are governed by permissions policies. An account administrator can attach permissions policies to IAM identities (that is, users, groups, and roles), as well as attaching permissions policies to resources.

Note

An *account administrator* (or administrator user) is a user with administrator privileges. For more information, see IAM Best Practices in the *IAM User Guide*.

When granting permissions, you decide who is getting the permissions, the resources they get permissions for, and the specific actions that you want to allow on those resources.

- AWS Migration Hub Resources and Operations
- Understanding Resource Ownership
- Managing Access to Resources
- Specifying Policy Elements: Actions, Effects, and Principals
- Specifying Conditions in a Policy

AWS Migration Hub Resources and Operations

In AWS Migration Hub, the primary resource is a Migration Hub *ProgressUpdateStream*. This resource has an unique Amazon Resource Name (ARN) associated with it as shown in the following table.

Resource Type	ARN Format
ProgressUpdateStream	arn:aws:mgh:*region*:*account-id*:ProgressUpdateStreamName:*resource-name*

AWS Migration Hub provides a set of operations to work with the Migration Hub resources. For a list of available operations, see Actions.

Understanding Resource Ownership

A *resource owner* is the AWS account that created the resource. That is, the resource owner is the AWS account of the *principal entity* (the root account, an IAM user, or an IAM role) that authenticates the request that creates the resource. The following examples illustrate how this works:

- If you use the root account credentials of your AWS account to create a Migration Hub ProgressUpdateStream, your AWS account is the owner of the resource (in Migration Hub, the resource is a ProgressUpdateStream).

- If you create an IAM user in your AWS account and grant permissions to create a Migration Hub ProgressUpdateStream to that user, the user can create a ProgressUpdateStream. However, your AWS account, to which the user belongs, owns the ProgressUpdateStream resource.

- If you create an IAM role in your AWS account with permissions to create a Migration Hub ProgressUpdateStream, anyone who can assume the role can create a ProgressUpdateStream. Your AWS account, to which the role belongs, owns the ProgressUpdateStream resource.

Managing Access to Resources

A *permissions policy* describes who has access to what. The following section explains the available options for creating permissions policies.

Note

This section discusses using IAM in the context of AWS Migration Hub. It doesn't provide detailed information about the IAM service. For complete IAM documentation, see What Is IAM? in the *IAM User Guide*. For information about IAM policy syntax and descriptions, see AWS IAM Policy Reference in the *IAM User Guide*.

Policies attached to an IAM identity are referred to as *identity-based* policies (IAM polices) and policies attached to a resource are referred to as *resource-based* policies. AWS Migration Hub *does not support resource-based policies*, see Resource-Based Policies.

- Identity-Based Policies (IAM Policies)
- Resource-Based Policies

Identity-Based Policies (IAM Policies)

You can attach policies to IAM identities. For example, you can do the following:

- **Attach a permissions policy to a user or a group in your account** – An account administrator can use a permissions policy that is associated with a particular user to grant permissions for that user to create a Migration Hub resource.

- **Attach a permissions policy to a role (grant cross-account permissions)** – You can attach an identity-based permissions policy to an IAM role to grant cross-account permissions. For example, the administrator in Account A can create a role to grant cross-account permissions to another AWS account (for example, Account B) or an AWS service as follows:

  1. Account A administrator creates an IAM role and attaches a permissions policy to the role that grants permissions on resources in Account A.

  2. Account A administrator attaches a trust policy to the role identifying Account B as the principal who can assume the role.

  3. Account B administrator can then delegate permissions to assume the role to any users in Account B. Doing this allows users in Account B to create or access resources in Account A. The principal in the trust policy can also be an AWS service principal if you want to grant an AWS service permissions to assume the role.

  For more information about using IAM to delegate permissions, see Access Management in the *IAM User Guide*.

The following is an example policy that grants permissions for the Migration Hub action `mgh:NotifyMigrationTaskState` on all resources.

```
1  {
2    "Version": "2017-03-31",
3    "Statement": {
4      "Effect": "Allow",
5      "Action":[
6        "mgh:NotifyMigrationTaskState"
7      ],
8      "Resource": "*"
9
10   }
11 }
```

For more information about using identity-based policies with Migration Hub, see Using Identity-Based Policies (IAM Policies) for AWS Migration Hub. For more information about users, groups, roles, and permissions, see Identities (Users, Groups, and Roles) in the *IAM User Guide*.

Resource-Based Policies

Other services, such as Amazon S3, also support resource-based permissions policies. For example, you can attach a policy to an S3 bucket to manage access permissions to that bucket. Migration Hub does not support resource-based policies. However, keep in mind that you will still see references made to resources. This is because there is a difference between *resource-based* permissions and *resource-level* permissions.

Resource-based permissions are permissions that attach directly to a resource, whereas a resource-level permission simply specifies, within an identity-based permission, on which resource an user or a role can perform actions on. Therefore, when references to resources are made discussing Migration Hub permissions, it is within this context of *resource-level* permissions.

Specifying Policy Elements: Actions, Effects, and Principals

For each Migration Hub resource, the service defines a set of API operations. To grant permissions for these API operations, Migration Hub defines a set of actions that you can specify in a policy. Some API operations can require permissions for more than one action in order to perform the API operation. For more information about resources and API operations, see AWS Migration Hub Resources and Operations and Migration Hub Actions.

The following are the most basic policy elements:

- **Resource** – You use an Amazon Resource Name (ARN) to identify the resource that the policy applies to. For more information, see AWS Migration Hub Resources and Operations.

- **Action** – You use action keywords to identify resource operations that you want to allow or deny. For example, you can use `mgh:AssociateDiscoveredResource` to allow the user permission to perform the Migration Hub `AssociateDiscoveredResource` operation.

- **Effect** – You specify the effect, either allow or deny, when the user requests the specific action. If you don't explicitly grant access to (allow) a resource, access is implicitly denied. You can also explicitly deny access to a resource, which you might do to make sure that a user cannot access it, even if a different policy grants access.

- **Principal** – In identity-based policies (IAM policies), the user that the policy is attached to is the implicit principal. For resource-based policies, you specify the user, account, service, or other entity that you want to receive permissions (applies to resource-based policies only). Migration Hub doesn't support resource-based policies.

To learn more about IAM policy syntax and descriptions, see AWS IAM Policy Reference in the *IAM User Guide*.

For a table showing all of the AWS Migration Hub API actions and the resources that they apply to, see AWS Migration Hub API Permissions: Actions and Resources Reference.

Specifying Conditions in a Policy

When you grant permissions, you can use the IAM policy language to specify the conditions when a policy should take effect. For example, you might want a policy to be applied only after a specific date. For more information about specifying conditions in a policy language, see Condition in the *IAM User Guide*.

To express conditions, you use predefined condition keys. There are no condition keys specific to Migration Hub. However, there are AWS-wide condition keys that you can use as appropriate. For a complete list of AWS-wide keys, see Available Keys for Conditions in the *IAM User Guide*.

Using Identity-Based Policies (IAM Policies) for AWS Migration Hub

This topic provides explanations of identity-based policies in which an account administrator can attach permissions policies to IAM identities (that is, users, groups, and roles).

Important
We recommend that you first review the introductory topics that explain the basic concepts and options available for you to manage access to your AWS Migration Hub resources. For more information, see Overview of Managing Access Permissions to Your AWS Migration Hub Resources.

The sections in this topic cover the following:

- Permissions Required to Use the AWS Migration Hub Console and API

- AWS Managed (Predefined) Policies for AWS Migration Hub

- AWS Migration Hub Trust Policies

The following shows an example of a permissions policy:

```
1  {
2      "Version": "2012-10-17",
3      "Statement": [
4          {
5              "Action": [
6                  "mgh:AssociateCreatedArtifact",
7                  "mgh:NotifyApplicationState",
8                  "mgh:ListDiscoveredResources"
9              ],
10             "Effect": "Allow",
11             "Resource": "arn:aws:mgh:us-west-2:account_num:ProgressUpdateStreamName/DMS/*"
12         }
13     ]
14 }
```

Next, you must define a trust policy that authorizes the migration tool, in this example, AWS Database Migration Service (DMS), to assume the role:

```
1  {
2    "Version": "2012-10-17",
3    "Statement": [
4      {
5        "Effect": "Allow",
6        "Principal": {
7          "Service": "dms.amazonaws.com"
8        },
9        "Action": "sts:AssumeRole"
10     }
11   ]
12 }
```

This policy is implemented in two parts, the permission policy and the trust policy:

- The permission policy grants permissions for the Migration Hub actions (mgh:AssociateCreatedArtifact, mgh:NotifyApplicationState, and mgh:ListDiscoveredResources) on any resources identified by the Amazon Resource Name (ARN) for the AWS DMS migration tool. The wildcard character (*) specified at the end of the resource name means that the migration tool can act on any migration tasks the tool creates under the particular ProgressUpdateStream name.

- The trust policy authorizes the AWS DMS migration tool to assume the role's permission policy. Migration Hub policies always require a trust policy to be associated with them.

For a table showing all of the AWS Migration Hub API actions and the resources and conditions that they apply to, see AWS Migration Hub API Permissions: Actions and Resources Reference.

Permissions Required to Use the AWS Migration Hub Console and API

The AWS Migration Hub console provides an integrated environment for users and APIs to create Migration Hub resources and to manage migrations. The console provides many features and workflows that require specific permissions in order to access. The best way to implement these permissions is through managed policies. See Console & API Managed Access.

In addition, there are API-specific permissions documented in AWS Migration Hub API Permissions: Actions and Resources Reference.

AWS Managed (Predefined) Policies for AWS Migration Hub

AWS addresses many common use cases by providing standalone IAM policies that are created and administered by AWS. These AWS managed policies grant necessary permissions for common use cases so that you can avoid having to investigate what permissions are needed.

The following AWS managed policies, which you can attach to users in your account, are specific to Migration Hub and are grouped by use case scenario:

- **AWSMigrationHubDiscoveryAccess** – Grants permission to allow the Migration Hub service to call Application Discovery Service.

- **AWSMigrationHubFullAccess** – Grants access to the Migration Hub console and API/CLI for an user who's not an administrator.

- **AWSMigrationHubSMSAccess** – Grants permission for Migration Hub to receive notifications from the AWS Server Migration Service migration tool.

- **AWSMigrationHubDMSAccess** – Grants permission for Migration Hub to receive notifications from the AWS Database Migration Service migration tool.

Note
You can review these permissions policies by signing in to the IAM console and searching for these specific policies there.

You can also create your own custom IAM policies to allow permissions for Migration Hub actions and resources. You can attach these custom policies to the IAM users or groups that require those permissions.

AWS Migration Hub Trust Policies

A trust policy simply authorizes the principal to assume, or use, the role's permission policy. A principal can be an AWS account (the "root" user), an IAM user, or a role. In Migration Hub, the trust policy must be manually added to the permission policy.

Therefore, each IAM role requires two separate policies that must be created for it:

- A permissions policy, which defines what actions and resources the principal is allowed to use.

- A trust policy, which specifies who is allowed to assume the role (the trusted entity, or principal).

Troubleshooting AWS Migration Hub

Following, you can find information on how to troubleshoot issues for AWS Migration Hub.

- My Migrations Do Not Appear in Migration Hub
- Updates About My Migrations Don't Appear Inside an Application

My Migrations Do Not Appear in Migration Hub

If you are not seeing your applications' migration status updates on the **Updates** page in Migration Hub, it is usually due to one of the following:

- Migration tools not being authorized to commmunicate with Migration Hub.

- You do not have the neccesary polices and roles set up in IAM.

- Migration status mapping is incorrect needs to be done manually.

Authentication

To make sure authentication is occurring correctly:

- Check if the migration tools you are using have been authorized to communicate with Migration Hub. For more information, see steps to authorize a migration tool.

- Check the Tools page to see the status of connected tools. Learn more about setting up necessary polices and roles in Required Managed Policies.

Migration Status Matching When Using AWS Discovery Tools

- Check if a migration update must be manually mapped or was incorrectly mapped to a discovered server, see Tracking Migration Updates.

Updates About My Migrations Don't Appear Inside an Application

If you are not seeing your migration updates associated with an application, it is usually due to one of the following:

- Servers not being grouped as an application.

- Migration update status not being refreshed.

- Migration updates are not mapped or are incorrectly mapped to a server.

Servers' Application Grouping

- Check if all your severs have been grouped into an application, see steps to groups servers into applications.

Update Status

- The application details page requires you to refresh the page in order to see the latest status. See steps to track status of migrations.

Update and Server Mapping

- Check if the update is present on **Updates** page.

- If not on the **Updates** page, then check if the migration tool was authorized by looking on the **Migration Tools** page - in the navigation pane, under **Migrate**, choose **Tools**.

- On the **Updates** page, verify the update is mapped to the correct server (will show "Edit" in "Mapped servers" column).

- If mapped to a server on the **Updates** page, then verify if the server is grouped into application on the **Servers** page with an application name present in the "Applications" column.

AWS Migration Hub API

The AWS Migration Hub API methods help to obtain server and application migration status and integrate your resource-specific migration tool by providing a programmatic interface to Migration Hub.

Reporting Migration Status Updates

Creating a `ProgressUpdateStream` for your Migration Tool

In order to send status to Migration Hub, you must first create a `ProgressUpdateStream` corresponding to your migration tool using `CreateProgressUpdateStream` and `ProgressUpdateStreamName` is the namespace for your migration tool. `ProgressUpdateStreamName` is scoped to the current AWS account, so it can be the same across all accounts. `ProgressUpdateStreamName` will be displayed as-is throughout the Migration Hub console as the name representing your migration tool. For example, Server Migration Service uses `ProgressUpdateStreamName` "SMS" and it is displayed as the "Migration Tool" on the application's page under the Migrate section.

Importing a Migration Task

Once you've created a `ProgressUpdateStream`, you can start importing migration tasks from your migration tool by calling `ImportMigrationTask`. It is recommended to call `ImportMigrationTask` as early as possible to inform the Migration Hub user about the existence of the task, even if the task has yet to be started.

Associating a Migration Task with a Previously Discovered Server

In order to add migration task detail to the console, the task must be associated with a resource. The resource represents the existing or source server for the migration. There are two ways that this association can be made:

- **Auto-mapping (recommended)**: A migration tool can associate (Put) sufficient identifiable information (e.g., IP address, MAC address, and/or fully qualified domain name, and in a VMware environment, vCenter ID, MoRef ID, VM name, and/or VM folder path) by calling `PutResourceAttributes` with a migration task so that AWS Migration Hub can correctly map the server being migrated to a server in AWS Application Discovery Service (ADS)'s servers repository. If Migration Hub does not find a matching server in ADS' server repository, then it automatically adds the server to the ADS repository.

- **Manual-mapping**: Alternatively, a migration tool can allow the user to make this association manually by providing them with a mapping experience within the migration tool's workflow that displays a list of existing AWS Application Discovery Service (ADS) servers. **Note**
This approach is not recommended and rarely necessary since auto-mapping (above) will automatically add and map the server from your tool to the Application Discovery Service repository when calling `PutResourceAttributes`.

Auto-Map Explained

- A migration tool uses the `PutResourceAttributes` API to provide information about the resource being migrated. This is done by an asynchronous association made with the resource after the `PutResourceAttributes` call is returned. If no matching server was found, then `PutResourceAttributes` automatically adds a server to the ADS repository and maps the migration task to the new server. This association can then be verified by calling `ListDiscoveredResource`.

- It is called with `MigrationTaskName` and `ResourceAttributes`. The `MigrationTaskName` is an identifier provided by the migration tool. This name uniquely identifies a migration task within your `ProgressUpdateStream`.

- The `ResourceAttributes` is descriptive information about the resource being migrated, such as a MAC address, IP address, fully qualified domain name, etc. for servers, or in a VMware environment, VM name, vCenter Id or MoRef ID. It can be used to associate the migration task with a server in the Application Discovery Service (ADS).

Sending Migration Status Updates

Now that a migration task exists, you can send migration status updates for display on the Migration Hub. Call AWS Migration Hub's `NotifyMigrationTaskState` API to share the latest task status. The information returned from this call contains the migration task's progress and status. This is the information that customers see displayed in Migration Hub.

The `MigrationTaskName` input parameter includes arguments used for addressing updates to the correct target task, and the `ProgressUpdateStream` parameter is used for access control and to provide a unique namespace scoped to the AWS account. API parameters are described in detail later in this section.

Migration Tool Expected Behavior

The following points are important information regarding the interaction between the migration tool you use and AWS Migration Hub.

- The migration tool is expected to retry on Migration Hub API failures.

- The migration tool is expected to publish updates as often as possible. A migration tool must specify its own update expectations with every call to `NotifyMigrationTaskState` API. It is recommended to send updates as soon as they are available.

- The migration tool should call `PutResourceAttributes`. If during the course of migration, the migration tool detects any change to the resource, or finds additional information, it can resend `PutResourceAttributes` data and Migration Hub will use the new values, overwriting old ones, and attempt to re-map to a resource in the Application Discovery Service.

API Endpoint

The API endpoint is the DNS name used as a host in the HTTP URI for the API calls. These API endpoints are region-specific and take the following form:

https://mgh/.us/-west/-2/.amazonaws/.com/

API Version

The version of the API being used for a call is identified by the first path segment of the request URI, and its form is a ISO 8601 date.

The documentation describes API version 2017-05-31.

AWS CloudTrail

Migration Hub is integrated with CloudTrail, a service that captures API calls from the Migration Hub console or from your code to the Migration Hub API operations. Using the information collected by CloudTrail, you can determine the request that was made to Migration Hub, the source IP address from which the request was made, who made the request, when it was made, and so on. See Logging AWS Migration Hub API Calls with AWS CloudTrail.

Related Topics

The following sections provide descriptions of the API operations, how to create a signature for request authentication, and how to grant permissions for these API operations using the IAM policies.

- Authentication and Access Control for AWS Migration Hub
- Actions
- Data Types
- AWS CloudTrail

Actions

The following actions are supported:

- AssociateCreatedArtifact
- AssociateDiscoveredResource
- CreateProgressUpdateStream
- DeleteProgressUpdateStream
- DescribeApplicationState
- DescribeMigrationTask
- DisassociateCreatedArtifact
- DisassociateDiscoveredResource
- ImportMigrationTask
- ListCreatedArtifacts
- ListDiscoveredResources
- ListMigrationTasks
- ListProgressUpdateStreams
- NotifyApplicationState
- NotifyMigrationTaskState
- PutResourceAttributes

AssociateCreatedArtifact

Associates a created artifact of an AWS cloud resource, the target receiving the migration, with the migration task performed by a migration tool. This API has the following traits:

- Migration tools can call the `AssociateCreatedArtifact` operation to indicate which AWS artifact is associated with a migration task.

- The created artifact name must be provided in ARN (Amazon Resource Name) format which will contain information about type and region; for example: `arn:aws:ec2:us-east-1:488216288981:image/ami-6d0ba87b`.

- Examples of the AWS resource behind the created artifact are, AMI's, EC2 instance, or DMS endpoint, etc.

Request Syntax

```
1 {
2    "[CreatedArtifact](#migrationhub-AssociateCreatedArtifact-request-CreatedArtifact)": {
3        "[Description](API_CreatedArtifact.md#migrationhub-Type-CreatedArtifact-Description)": "
            string",
4        "[Name](API_CreatedArtifact.md#migrationhub-Type-CreatedArtifact-Name)": "string"
5    },
6    "[DryRun](#migrationhub-AssociateCreatedArtifact-request-DryRun)": boolean,
7    "[MigrationTaskName](#migrationhub-AssociateCreatedArtifact-request-MigrationTaskName)": "
            string",
8    "[ProgressUpdateStream](#migrationhub-AssociateCreatedArtifact-request-ProgressUpdateStream)
            ": "string"
9 }
```

Request Parameters

The request accepts the following data in JSON format.

** CreatedArtifact ** An ARN of the AWS resource related to the migration (e.g., AMI, EC2 instance, RDS instance, etc.)
Type: CreatedArtifact object
Required: Yes

** DryRun ** Optional boolean flag to indicate whether any effect should take place. Used to test if the caller has permission to make the call.
Type: Boolean
Required: No

** MigrationTaskName ** Unique identifier that references the migration task.
Type: String
Length Constraints: Minimum length of 1. Maximum length of 256.
Pattern: `[^:|]+`
Required: Yes

** ProgressUpdateStream ** The name of the ProgressUpdateStream.
Type: String
Length Constraints: Minimum length of 1. Maximum length of 50.
Pattern: `[^/:|\000-\037]+`
Required: Yes

Response Elements

If the action is successful, the service sends back an HTTP 200 response with an empty HTTP body.

Errors

AccessDeniedException
You do not have sufficient access to perform this action.
HTTP Status Code: 400

DryRunOperation
Exception raised to indicate a successfully authorized action when the DryRun flag is set to "true".
HTTP Status Code: 400

InternalServerError
Exception raised when there is an internal, configuration, or dependency error encountered.
HTTP Status Code: 500

InvalidInputException
Exception raised when the provided input violates a policy constraint or is entered in the wrong format or data type.
HTTP Status Code: 400

ResourceNotFoundException
Exception raised when the request references a resource (ADS configuration, update stream, migration task, etc.) that does not exist in ADS (Application Discovery Service) or in Migration Hub's repository.
HTTP Status Code: 400

ServiceUnavailableException
Exception raised when there is an internal, configuration, or dependency error encountered.
HTTP Status Code: 500

UnauthorizedOperation
Exception raised to indicate a request was not authorized when the DryRun flag is set to "true".
HTTP Status Code: 400

Example

Associate a created artifact

The following example associates an AWS resource to the migration task identified by the values passed to the required parameters of `MigrationTaskName` and `ProgressUpdateStream` in the request.

Sample Request

```
1  {
2     "CreatedArtifact": [
3        {
4           "Description": "Using SMS to migrate server to EC2",
5           "Name": "arn:aws:ec2:us-east-1:488216288981:image/ami-6d0ba87b"
6        }
7     ],
8     "DryRun": false,
9     "MigrationTaskName": "sms-12de3cf1a",
10    "ProgressUpdateStream": "SMS"
```

```
11
12 }
```

See Also

For more information about using this API in one of the language-specific AWS SDKs, see the following:

- AWS Command Line Interface
- AWS SDK for .NET
- AWS SDK for C++
- AWS SDK for Go
- AWS SDK for Java
- AWS SDK for JavaScript
- AWS SDK for PHP V3
- AWS SDK for Python
- AWS SDK for Ruby V2

AssociateDiscoveredResource

Associates a discovered resource ID from Application Discovery Service (ADS) with a migration task.

Request Syntax

```
1 {
2    "[DiscoveredResource](#migrationhub-AssociateDiscoveredResource-request-DiscoveredResource)":
         {
3       "[ConfigurationId](API_DiscoveredResource.md#migrationhub-Type-DiscoveredResource-
            ConfigurationId)": "string",
4       "[Description](API_DiscoveredResource.md#migrationhub-Type-DiscoveredResource-Description)
            ": "string"
5    },
6    "[DryRun](#migrationhub-AssociateDiscoveredResource-request-DryRun)": boolean,
7    "[MigrationTaskName](#migrationhub-AssociateDiscoveredResource-request-MigrationTaskName)": "
         string",
8    "[ProgressUpdateStream](#migrationhub-AssociateDiscoveredResource-request-
         ProgressUpdateStream)": "string"
9 }
```

Request Parameters

The request accepts the following data in JSON format.

** DiscoveredResource ** Object representing a Resource.
Type: DiscoveredResource object
Required: Yes

** DryRun ** Optional boolean flag to indicate whether any effect should take place. Used to test if the caller has permission to make the call.
Type: Boolean
Required: No

** MigrationTaskName ** The identifier given to the MigrationTask.
Type: String
Length Constraints: Minimum length of 1. Maximum length of 256.
Pattern: [^:|]+
Required: Yes

** ProgressUpdateStream ** The name of the ProgressUpdateStream.
Type: String
Length Constraints: Minimum length of 1. Maximum length of 50.
Pattern: [^/:|\000-\037]+
Required: Yes

Response Elements

If the action is successful, the service sends back an HTTP 200 response with an empty HTTP body.

Errors

AccessDeniedException
You do not have sufficient access to perform this action.
HTTP Status Code: 400

DryRunOperation
Exception raised to indicate a successfully authorized action when the `DryRun` flag is set to "true".
HTTP Status Code: 400

InternalServerError
Exception raised when there is an internal, configuration, or dependency error encountered.
HTTP Status Code: 500

InvalidInputException
Exception raised when the provided input violates a policy constraint or is entered in the wrong format or data type.
HTTP Status Code: 400

PolicyErrorException
Exception raised when there are problems accessing ADS (Application Discovery Service); most likely due to a misconfigured policy or the `migrationhub-discovery` role is missing or not configured correctly.
HTTP Status Code: 400

ResourceNotFoundException
Exception raised when the request references a resource (ADS configuration, update stream, migration task, etc.) that does not exist in ADS (Application Discovery Service) or in Migration Hub's repository.
HTTP Status Code: 400

ServiceUnavailableException
Exception raised when there is an internal, configuration, or dependency error encountered.
HTTP Status Code: 500

UnauthorizedOperation
Exception raised to indicate a request was not authorized when the `DryRun` flag is set to "true".
HTTP Status Code: 400

Example

Associate a discovered resource

The following example associates an AWS Application Discovery Service (ADS) discovered resource specified by its configuration id and description to the migration task identified by the values passed to the required parameters of `MigrationTaskName` and `ProgressUpdateStream` in the request.

Sample Request

```
1 {
2     "ProgressUpdateStream": "SMS",
3     "MigrationTaskName": "sms-12de3cf1a",
4     "DiscoveredResource": {
5         "ConfigurationId": "d-server-0025db43a885966c8",
6         "Description": "Amazon Linux AMI release 2016.09"
7     }
8 }
```

See Also

For more information about using this API in one of the language-specific AWS SDKs, see the following:

- AWS Command Line Interface
- AWS SDK for .NET
- AWS SDK for C++
- AWS SDK for Go
- AWS SDK for Java
- AWS SDK for JavaScript
- AWS SDK for PHP V3
- AWS SDK for Python
- AWS SDK for Ruby V2

CreateProgressUpdateStream

Creates a progress update stream which is an AWS resource used for access control as well as a namespace for migration task names that is implicitly linked to your AWS account. It must uniquely identify the migration tool as it is used for all updates made by the tool; however, it does not need to be unique for each AWS account because it is scoped to the AWS account.

Request Syntax

```
1 {
2    "[DryRun](#migrationhub-CreateProgressUpdateStream-request-DryRun)": boolean,
3    "[ProgressUpdateStreamName](#migrationhub-CreateProgressUpdateStream-request-
       ProgressUpdateStreamName)": "string"
4 }
```

Request Parameters

The request accepts the following data in JSON format.

** DryRun ** Optional boolean flag to indicate whether any effect should take place. Used to test if the caller has permission to make the call.
Type: Boolean
Required: No

** ProgressUpdateStreamName ** The name of the ProgressUpdateStream.
Type: String
Length Constraints: Minimum length of 1. Maximum length of 50.
Pattern: [^/:|\000-\037]+
Required: Yes

Response Elements

If the action is successful, the service sends back an HTTP 200 response with an empty HTTP body.

Errors

AccessDeniedException
You do not have sufficient access to perform this action.
HTTP Status Code: 400

DryRunOperation
Exception raised to indicate a successfully authorized action when the DryRun flag is set to "true".
HTTP Status Code: 400

InternalServerError
Exception raised when there is an internal, configuration, or dependency error encountered.
HTTP Status Code: 500

InvalidInputException
Exception raised when the provided input violates a policy constraint or is entered in the wrong format or data type.
HTTP Status Code: 400

ServiceUnavailableException

Exception raised when there is an internal, configuration, or dependency error encountered.
HTTP Status Code: 500

UnauthorizedOperation

Exception raised to indicate a request was not authorized when the `DryRun` flag is set to "true".
HTTP Status Code: 400

Example

Create a progress update stream

The following example creates a progress update stream identified by the values passed to the required parameter `ProgressUpdateStreamName` in the request.

Sample Request

```
1 {
2     "ProgressUpdateStreamName": "SMS",
3     "DryRun": false
4 }
```

See Also

For more information about using this API in one of the language-specific AWS SDKs, see the following:

- AWS Command Line Interface
- AWS SDK for .NET
- AWS SDK for C++
- AWS SDK for Go
- AWS SDK for Java
- AWS SDK for JavaScript
- AWS SDK for PHP V3
- AWS SDK for Python
- AWS SDK for Ruby V2

DeleteProgressUpdateStream

Deletes a progress update stream, including all of its tasks, which was previously created as an AWS resource used for access control. This API has the following traits:

- The only parameter needed for `DeleteProgressUpdateStream` is the stream name (same as a `CreateProgressUpdateStream` call).

- The call will return, and a background process will asynchronously delete the stream and all of its resources (tasks, associated resources, resource attributes, created artifacts).

- If the stream takes time to be deleted, it might still show up on a `ListProgressUpdateStreams` call.

- `CreateProgressUpdateStream`, `ImportMigrationTask`, `NotifyMigrationTaskState`, and all Associate[*] APIs realted to the tasks belonging to the stream will throw "InvalidInputException" if the stream of the same name is in the process of being deleted.

- Once the stream and all of its resources are deleted, `CreateProgressUpdateStream` for a stream of the same name will succeed, and that stream will be an entirely new logical resource (without any resources associated with the old stream).

Request Syntax

```
1 {
2    "[DryRun](#migrationhub-DeleteProgressUpdateStream-request-DryRun)": boolean,
3    "[ProgressUpdateStreamName](#migrationhub-DeleteProgressUpdateStream-request-
         ProgressUpdateStreamName)": "string"
4 }
```

Request Parameters

The request accepts the following data in JSON format.

** DryRun ** Optional boolean flag to indicate whether any effect should take place. Used to test if the caller has permission to make the call.
Type: Boolean
Required: No

** ProgressUpdateStreamName ** The name of the ProgressUpdateStream.
Type: String
Length Constraints: Minimum length of 1. Maximum length of 50.
Pattern: `[^/:|\000-\037]+`
Required: Yes

Response Elements

If the action is successful, the service sends back an HTTP 200 response with an empty HTTP body.

Errors

AccessDeniedException
You do not have sufficient access to perform this action.
HTTP Status Code: 400

DryRunOperation
Exception raised to indicate a successfully authorized action when the `DryRun` flag is set to "true".
HTTP Status Code: 400

InternalServerError
Exception raised when there is an internal, configuration, or dependency error encountered.
HTTP Status Code: 500

InvalidInputException
Exception raised when the provided input violates a policy constraint or is entered in the wrong format or data type.
HTTP Status Code: 400

ResourceNotFoundException
Exception raised when the request references a resource (ADS configuration, update stream, migration task, etc.) that does not exist in ADS (Application Discovery Service) or in Migration Hub's repository.
HTTP Status Code: 400

ServiceUnavailableException
Exception raised when there is an internal, configuration, or dependency error encountered.
HTTP Status Code: 500

UnauthorizedOperation
Exception raised to indicate a request was not authorized when the `DryRun` flag is set to "true".
HTTP Status Code: 400

Example

Delete a progress update stream

The following example deletes a progress update stream identified by the values passed to the required parameter `ProgressUpdateStreamName` in the request.

Sample Request

```
1 {
2     "ProgressUpdateStreamName": "SMS",
3     "DryRun": false
4 }
```

See Also

For more information about using this API in one of the language-specific AWS SDKs, see the following:

- AWS Command Line Interface
- AWS SDK for .NET
- AWS SDK for C++
- AWS SDK for Go
- AWS SDK for Java
- AWS SDK for JavaScript
- AWS SDK for PHP V3
- AWS SDK for Python

- AWS SDK for Ruby V2

DescribeApplicationState

Gets the migration status of an application.

Request Syntax

```
1 {
2     "[ApplicationId](#migrationhub-DescribeApplicationState-request-ApplicationId)": "string"
3 }
```

Request Parameters

The request accepts the following data in JSON format.

** ApplicationId ** The configurationId in ADS that uniquely identifies the grouped application.
Type: String
Length Constraints: Minimum length of 1. Maximum length of 1600.
Required: Yes

Response Syntax

```
1 {
2     "[ApplicationStatus](#migrationhub-DescribeApplicationState-response-ApplicationStatus)": "
        string",
3     "[LastUpdatedTime](#migrationhub-DescribeApplicationState-response-LastUpdatedTime)": number
4 }
```

Response Elements

If the action is successful, the service sends back an HTTP 200 response.

The following data is returned in JSON format by the service.

** ApplicationStatus ** Status of the application - Not Started, In-Progress, Complete.
Type: String
Valid Values:NOT_STARTED | IN_PROGRESS | COMPLETED

** LastUpdatedTime ** The timestamp when the application status was last updated.
Type: Timestamp

Errors

AccessDeniedException
You do not have sufficient access to perform this action.
HTTP Status Code: 400

InternalServerError
Exception raised when there is an internal, configuration, or dependency error encountered.
HTTP Status Code: 500

InvalidInputException
Exception raised when the provided input violates a policy constraint or is entered in the wrong format or data type.
HTTP Status Code: 400

PolicyErrorException

Exception raised when there are problems accessing ADS (Application Discovery Service); most likely due to a misconfigured policy or the `migrationhub-discovery` role is missing or not configured correctly.
HTTP Status Code: 400

ResourceNotFoundException

Exception raised when the request references a resource (ADS configuration, update stream, migration task, etc.) that does not exist in ADS (Application Discovery Service) or in Migration Hub's repository.
HTTP Status Code: 400

ServiceUnavailableException

Exception raised when there is an internal, configuration, or dependency error encountered.
HTTP Status Code: 500

Example

Describe a migration task by listing all associated attributes

The following example lists all of the attributes associated with the values passed to the required parameters of `MigrationTaskName` and `ProgressUpdateStream`.

Sample Request

```
1 {
2     "ApplicationId": "d-application-0039038d504694533"
3 }
```

Sample Response

```
1 {
2     "ApplicationStatus": "IN_PROGRESS",
3     "LastUpdatedTime": 1493405005.639
4 }
```

See Also

For more information about using this API in one of the language-specific AWS SDKs, see the following:

- AWS Command Line Interface
- AWS SDK for .NET
- AWS SDK for C++
- AWS SDK for Go
- AWS SDK for Java
- AWS SDK for JavaScript
- AWS SDK for PHP V3
- AWS SDK for Python
- AWS SDK for Ruby V2

DescribeMigrationTask

Retrieves a list of all attributes associated with a specific migration task.

Request Syntax

```
1 {
2    "[MigrationTaskName](#migrationhub-DescribeMigrationTask-request-MigrationTaskName)": "string
        ",
3    "[ProgressUpdateStream](#migrationhub-DescribeMigrationTask-request-ProgressUpdateStream)": "
        string"
4 }
```

Request Parameters

The request accepts the following data in JSON format.

** MigrationTaskName ** The identifier given to the MigrationTask.
Type: String
Length Constraints: Minimum length of 1. Maximum length of 256.
Pattern: [^:|]+
Required: Yes

** ProgressUpdateStream ** The name of the ProgressUpdateStream.
Type: String
Length Constraints: Minimum length of 1. Maximum length of 50.
Pattern: [^/:|\000-\037]+
Required: Yes

Response Syntax

```
1 {
2    "[MigrationTask](#migrationhub-DescribeMigrationTask-response-MigrationTask)": {
3       "[MigrationTaskName](API_MigrationTask.md#migrationhub-Type-MigrationTask-
           MigrationTaskName)": "string",
4       "[ProgressUpdateStream](API_MigrationTask.md#migrationhub-Type-MigrationTask-
           ProgressUpdateStream)": "string",
5       "[ResourceAttributeList](API_MigrationTask.md#migrationhub-Type-MigrationTask-
           ResourceAttributeList)": [
6          {
7             "[Type](API_ResourceAttribute.md#migrationhub-Type-ResourceAttribute-Type)": "string
                 ",
8             "[Value](API_ResourceAttribute.md#migrationhub-Type-ResourceAttribute-Value)": "
                 string"
9          }
10      ],
11      "[Task](API_MigrationTask.md#migrationhub-Type-MigrationTask-Task)": {
12         "[ProgressPercent](API_Task.md#migrationhub-Type-Task-ProgressPercent)": number,
13         "[Status](API_Task.md#migrationhub-Type-Task-Status)": "string",
14         "[StatusDetail](API_Task.md#migrationhub-Type-Task-StatusDetail)": "string"
15      },
16      "[UpdateDateTime](API_MigrationTask.md#migrationhub-Type-MigrationTask-UpdateDateTime)":
           number
```

```
17      }
18 }
```

Response Elements

If the action is successful, the service sends back an HTTP 200 response.

The following data is returned in JSON format by the service.

** MigrationTask ** Object encapsulating information about the migration task.
Type: MigrationTask object

Errors

AccessDeniedException
You do not have sufficient access to perform this action.
HTTP Status Code: 400

InternalServerError
Exception raised when there is an internal, configuration, or dependency error encountered.
HTTP Status Code: 500

InvalidInputException
Exception raised when the provided input violates a policy constraint or is entered in the wrong format or data type.
HTTP Status Code: 400

ResourceNotFoundException
Exception raised when the request references a resource (ADS configuration, update stream, migration task, etc.) that does not exist in ADS (Application Discovery Service) or in Migration Hub's repository.
HTTP Status Code: 400

ServiceUnavailableException
Exception raised when there is an internal, configuration, or dependency error encountered.
HTTP Status Code: 500

Example

Describe a migration task by listing all associated attributes

The following example lists all of the attributes associated with the values passed to the required parameters of `MigrationTaskName` and `ProgressUpdateStream`.

Sample Request

```
1 {
2     "ProgressUpdateStream": "SMS",
3     "MigrationTaskName": "sms-12de3cf1a"
4 }
```

Sample Response

```
1  {
2      "MigrationTask": {
3          "ProgressUpdateStream": "SMS",
4          "Task": {
5              "Status": "IN_PROGRESS",
6              "StatusDetail": "Migration: Copying image data",
7              "ProgressPercent": 77
8          },
9          "UpdateDateTime": 1493750385.0,
10         "MigrationTaskName": "sms-12de3cf1a"
11     }
12 }
```

See Also

For more information about using this API in one of the language-specific AWS SDKs, see the following:

- AWS Command Line Interface
- AWS SDK for .NET
- AWS SDK for C++
- AWS SDK for Go
- AWS SDK for Java
- AWS SDK for JavaScript
- AWS SDK for PHP V3
- AWS SDK for Python
- AWS SDK for Ruby V2

DisassociateCreatedArtifact

Disassociates a created artifact of an AWS resource with a migration task performed by a migration tool that was previously associated. This API has the following traits:

- A migration user can call the `DisassociateCreatedArtifacts` operation to disassociate a created AWS Artifact from a migration task.

- The created artifact name must be provided in ARN (Amazon Resource Name) format which will contain information about type and region; for example: `arn:aws:ec2:us-east-1:488216288981:image/ami-6d0ba87b`.

- Examples of the AWS resource behind the created artifact are, AMI's, EC2 instance, or RDS instance, etc.

Request Syntax

```
1  {
2      "[CreatedArtifactName](#migrationhub-DisassociateCreatedArtifact-request-CreatedArtifactName)": "string",
3      "[DryRun](#migrationhub-DisassociateCreatedArtifact-request-DryRun)": boolean,
4      "[MigrationTaskName](#migrationhub-DisassociateCreatedArtifact-request-MigrationTaskName)": "string",
5      "[ProgressUpdateStream](#migrationhub-DisassociateCreatedArtifact-request-ProgressUpdateStream)": "string"
6  }
```

Request Parameters

The request accepts the following data in JSON format.

** CreatedArtifactName ** An ARN of the AWS resource related to the migration (e.g., AMI, EC2 instance, RDS instance, etc.)
Type: String
Length Constraints: Minimum length of 1. Maximum length of 1600.
Pattern: `arn:[a-z-]+:[a-z0-9-]+:(?:[a-z0-9-]+|):(?:[0-9]{12}|):.*`
Required: Yes

** DryRun ** Optional boolean flag to indicate whether any effect should take place. Used to test if the caller has permission to make the call.
Type: Boolean
Required: No

** MigrationTaskName ** Unique identifier that references the migration task to be disassociated with the artifact.
Type: String
Length Constraints: Minimum length of 1. Maximum length of 256.
Pattern: `[^:|]+`
Required: Yes

** ProgressUpdateStream ** The name of the ProgressUpdateStream.
Type: String
Length Constraints: Minimum length of 1. Maximum length of 50.
Pattern: `[^/:|\000-\037]+`
Required: Yes

Response Elements

If the action is successful, the service sends back an HTTP 200 response with an empty HTTP body.

Errors

AccessDeniedException
You do not have sufficient access to perform this action.
HTTP Status Code: 400

DryRunOperation
Exception raised to indicate a successfully authorized action when the `DryRun` flag is set to "true".
HTTP Status Code: 400

InternalServerError
Exception raised when there is an internal, configuration, or dependency error encountered.
HTTP Status Code: 500

InvalidInputException
Exception raised when the provided input violates a policy constraint or is entered in the wrong format or data type.
HTTP Status Code: 400

ResourceNotFoundException
Exception raised when the request references a resource (ADS configuration, update stream, migration task, etc.) that does not exist in ADS (Application Discovery Service) or in Migration Hub's repository.
HTTP Status Code: 400

ServiceUnavailableException
Exception raised when there is an internal, configuration, or dependency error encountered.
HTTP Status Code: 500

UnauthorizedOperation
Exception raised to indicate a request was not authorized when the `DryRun` flag is set to "true".
HTTP Status Code: 400

Example

Disassociate a created artifact

The following example disassociates an AWS resource from the migration task `d-server-0025db43a885966c8` using its ARN formatted name `geaws:ec2:us-east-1:488216288981:image/ami-6d0ba87b`.

Sample Request

```
1 {
2     "CreatedArtifactName": "arn:aws:ec2:us-east-1:488216288981:image/ami-6d0ba87b",
3     "MigrationTaskName": "sms-12de3cf1a",
4     "ProgressUpdateStream": "SMS"
5 }
```

See Also

For more information about using this API in one of the language-specific AWS SDKs, see the following:

- AWS Command Line Interface
- AWS SDK for .NET
- AWS SDK for C++
- AWS SDK for Go
- AWS SDK for Java
- AWS SDK for JavaScript
- AWS SDK for PHP V3
- AWS SDK for Python
- AWS SDK for Ruby V2

DisassociateDiscoveredResource

Disassociate an Application Discovery Service (ADS) discovered resource from a migration task.

Request Syntax

```
1 {
2    "[ConfigurationId](#migrationhub-DisassociateDiscoveredResource-request-ConfigurationId)": "
        string",
3    "[DryRun](#migrationhub-DisassociateDiscoveredResource-request-DryRun)": boolean,
4    "[MigrationTaskName](#migrationhub-DisassociateDiscoveredResource-request-MigrationTaskName)
        ": "string",
5    "[ProgressUpdateStream](#migrationhub-DisassociateDiscoveredResource-request-
        ProgressUpdateStream)": "string"
6 }
```

Request Parameters

The request accepts the following data in JSON format.

** ConfigurationId ** ConfigurationId of the ADS resource to be disassociated.
Type: String
Length Constraints: Minimum length of 1.
Required: Yes

** DryRun ** Optional boolean flag to indicate whether any effect should take place. Used to test if the caller has permission to make the call.
Type: Boolean
Required: No

** MigrationTaskName ** The identifier given to the MigrationTask.
Type: String
Length Constraints: Minimum length of 1. Maximum length of 256.
Pattern: [^:|]+
Required: Yes

** ProgressUpdateStream ** The name of the ProgressUpdateStream.
Type: String
Length Constraints: Minimum length of 1. Maximum length of 50.
Pattern: [^/:|\000-\037]+
Required: Yes

Response Elements

If the action is successful, the service sends back an HTTP 200 response with an empty HTTP body.

Errors

AccessDeniedException
You do not have sufficient access to perform this action.
HTTP Status Code: 400

DryRunOperation

Exception raised to indicate a successfully authorized action when the `DryRun` flag is set to "true".
HTTP Status Code: 400

InternalServerError

Exception raised when there is an internal, configuration, or dependency error encountered.
HTTP Status Code: 500

InvalidInputException

Exception raised when the provided input violates a policy constraint or is entered in the wrong format or data type.
HTTP Status Code: 400

ResourceNotFoundException

Exception raised when the request references a resource (ADS configuration, update stream, migration task, etc.) that does not exist in ADS (Application Discovery Service) or in Migration Hub's repository.
HTTP Status Code: 400

ServiceUnavailableException

Exception raised when there is an internal, configuration, or dependency error encountered.
HTTP Status Code: 500

UnauthorizedOperation

Exception raised to indicate a request was not authorized when the `DryRun` flag is set to "true".
HTTP Status Code: 400

Example

Disassociate a discovered resource from the repository

The following example removes the association between the ADS `ConfigurationId` and the `MigrationTaskName` by passing its name value to the required parameter `ConfigurationId` as well as the required parameters `MigrationTaskName` and `ProgressUpdateStreamName` which specify the created artifact to disassociate from.

Sample Request

```
1 {
2     "DryRun": false,
3     "MigrationTaskName": "sms-12de3cf1a",
4     "ProgressUpdateStream": "SMS",
5     "ConfigurationId": "d-server-0025db43a885966c8"
6 }
```

See Also

For more information about using this API in one of the language-specific AWS SDKs, see the following:

- AWS Command Line Interface
- AWS SDK for .NET
- AWS SDK for C++
- AWS SDK for Go
- AWS SDK for Java
- AWS SDK for JavaScript

- AWS SDK for PHP V3
- AWS SDK for Python
- AWS SDK for Ruby V2

ImportMigrationTask

Registers a new migration task which represents a server, database, etc., being migrated to AWS by a migration tool.

This API is a prerequisite to calling the `NotifyMigrationTaskState` API as the migration tool must first register the migration task with Migration Hub.

Request Syntax

```
1 {
2   "[DryRun](#migrationhub-ImportMigrationTask-request-DryRun)": boolean,
3   "[MigrationTaskName](#migrationhub-ImportMigrationTask-request-MigrationTaskName)": "string",
4   "[ProgressUpdateStream](#migrationhub-ImportMigrationTask-request-ProgressUpdateStream)": "
       string"
5 }
```

Request Parameters

The request accepts the following data in JSON format.

** DryRun ** Optional boolean flag to indicate whether any effect should take place. Used to test if the caller has permission to make the call.
Type: Boolean
Required: No

** MigrationTaskName ** Unique identifier that references the migration task.
Type: String
Length Constraints: Minimum length of 1. Maximum length of 256.
Pattern: [^:|]+
Required: Yes

** ProgressUpdateStream ** The name of the ProgressUpdateStream.
Type: String
Length Constraints: Minimum length of 1. Maximum length of 50.
Pattern: [^/:|\000-\037]+
Required: Yes

Response Elements

If the action is successful, the service sends back an HTTP 200 response with an empty HTTP body.

Errors

AccessDeniedException
You do not have sufficient access to perform this action.
HTTP Status Code: 400

DryRunOperation
Exception raised to indicate a successfully authorized action when the `DryRun` flag is set to "true".
HTTP Status Code: 400

InternalServerError

Exception raised when there is an internal, configuration, or dependency error encountered.
HTTP Status Code: 500

InvalidInputException

Exception raised when the provided input violates a policy constraint or is entered in the wrong format or data type.
HTTP Status Code: 400

ResourceNotFoundException

Exception raised when the request references a resource (ADS configuration, update stream, migration task, etc.) that does not exist in ADS (Application Discovery Service) or in Migration Hub's repository.
HTTP Status Code: 400

ServiceUnavailableException

Exception raised when there is an internal, configuration, or dependency error encountered.
HTTP Status Code: 500

UnauthorizedOperation

Exception raised to indicate a request was not authorized when the `DryRun` flag is set to "true".
HTTP Status Code: 400

Example

Import a migration task to register it with Migration Hub

The following example registers a new migration task with Migration Hub identified by the values passed to the required parameters `MigrationTaskName` and `ProgressUpdateStreamName` in the request.

Sample Request

```
1 {
2     "MigrationTaskName": "sms-12de3cf1a",
3     "ProgressUpdateStream": "SMS"
4 }
```

See Also

For more information about using this API in one of the language-specific AWS SDKs, see the following:

- AWS Command Line Interface

- AWS SDK for .NET

- AWS SDK for C++

- AWS SDK for Go

- AWS SDK for Java

- AWS SDK for JavaScript

- AWS SDK for PHP V3

- AWS SDK for Python

- AWS SDK for Ruby V2

ListCreatedArtifacts

Lists the created artifacts attached to a given migration task in an update stream. This API has the following traits:

- Gets the list of the created artifacts while migration is taking place.

- Shows the artifacts created by the migration tool that was associated by the `AssociateCreatedArtifact` API.

- Lists created artifacts in a paginated interface.

Request Syntax

```
1 {
2    "[MaxResults](#migrationhub-ListCreatedArtifacts-request-MaxResults)": number,
3    "[MigrationTaskName](#migrationhub-ListCreatedArtifacts-request-MigrationTaskName)": "string
       ",
4    "[NextToken](#migrationhub-ListCreatedArtifacts-request-NextToken)": "string",
5    "[ProgressUpdateStream](#migrationhub-ListCreatedArtifacts-request-ProgressUpdateStream)": "
       string"
6 }
```

Request Parameters

The request accepts the following data in JSON format.

** MaxResults ** Maximum number of results to be returned per page.
Type: Integer
Valid Range: Minimum value of 1. Maximum value of 10.
Required: No

** MigrationTaskName ** Unique identifier that references the migration task.
Type: String
Length Constraints: Minimum length of 1. Maximum length of 256.
Pattern: [^:|]+
Required: Yes

** NextToken ** If a `NextToken` was returned by a previous call, there are more results available. To retrieve the next page of results, make the call again using the returned token in `NextToken`.
Type: String
Required: No

** ProgressUpdateStream ** The name of the ProgressUpdateStream.
Type: String
Length Constraints: Minimum length of 1. Maximum length of 50.
Pattern: [^/:|\000-\037]+
Required: Yes

Response Syntax

```
1 {
2    "[CreatedArtifactList](#migrationhub-ListCreatedArtifacts-response-CreatedArtifactList)": [
3       {
```

```
4        "[Description](API_CreatedArtifact.md#migrationhub-Type-CreatedArtifact-Description)":
             "string",
5        "[Name](API_CreatedArtifact.md#migrationhub-Type-CreatedArtifact-Name)": "string"
6      }
7    ],
8    "[NextToken](#migrationhub-ListCreatedArtifacts-response-NextToken)": "string"
9  }
```

Response Elements

If the action is successful, the service sends back an HTTP 200 response.

The following data is returned in JSON format by the service.

** CreatedArtifactList ** List of created artifacts up to the maximum number of results specified in the request.
Type: Array of CreatedArtifact objects

** NextToken ** If there are more created artifacts than the max result, return the next token to be passed to the next call as a bookmark of where to start from.
Type: String

Errors

AccessDeniedException
You do not have sufficient access to perform this action.
HTTP Status Code: 400

InternalServerError
Exception raised when there is an internal, configuration, or dependency error encountered.
HTTP Status Code: 500

InvalidInputException
Exception raised when the provided input violates a policy constraint or is entered in the wrong format or data type.
HTTP Status Code: 400

ResourceNotFoundException
Exception raised when the request references a resource (ADS configuration, update stream, migration task, etc.) that does not exist in ADS (Application Discovery Service) or in Migration Hub's repository.
HTTP Status Code: 400

ServiceUnavailableException
Exception raised when there is an internal, configuration, or dependency error encountered.
HTTP Status Code: 500

Example

List created artifacts associated with a migration task and update stream

The following example lists the created artifact name and its description that is associated with the values passed to the required parameters of `MigrationTaskName` and `ProgressUpdateStream` in the request.

Sample Request

```
1 {
2     "ProgressUpdateStream": "SMS",
3     "MigrationTaskName": "sms-12de3cf1a",
4     "MaxResults": 1
5 }
```

Sample Response

```
1 {
2     "CreatedArtifactList": [
3         {
4             "Name": "arn:aws:ec2:us-east-1:488216288981:image/ami-6d0ba87b",
5             "Description": "Using SMS to migrate server to EC2"
6         }
7     ]
8 }
```

See Also

For more information about using this API in one of the language-specific AWS SDKs, see the following:

- AWS Command Line Interface
- AWS SDK for .NET
- AWS SDK for C++
- AWS SDK for Go
- AWS SDK for Java
- AWS SDK for JavaScript
- AWS SDK for PHP V3
- AWS SDK for Python
- AWS SDK for Ruby V2

ListDiscoveredResources

Lists discovered resources associated with the given `MigrationTask`.

Request Syntax

```
1 {
2    "[MaxResults](#migrationhub-ListDiscoveredResources-request-MaxResults)": number,
3    "[MigrationTaskName](#migrationhub-ListDiscoveredResources-request-MigrationTaskName)": "
         string",
4    "[NextToken](#migrationhub-ListDiscoveredResources-request-NextToken)": "string",
5    "[ProgressUpdateStream](#migrationhub-ListDiscoveredResources-request-ProgressUpdateStream)":
         "string"
6 }
```

Request Parameters

The request accepts the following data in JSON format.

** MaxResults ** The maximum number of results returned per page.
Type: Integer
Valid Range: Minimum value of 1. Maximum value of 10.
Required: No

** MigrationTaskName ** The name of the MigrationTask.
Type: String
Length Constraints: Minimum length of 1. Maximum length of 256.
Pattern: [^:|]+
Required: Yes

** NextToken ** If a `NextToken` was returned by a previous call, there are more results available. To retrieve the next page of results, make the call again using the returned token in `NextToken`.
Type: String
Required: No

** ProgressUpdateStream ** The name of the ProgressUpdateStream.
Type: String
Length Constraints: Minimum length of 1. Maximum length of 50.
Pattern: [^/:|\000-\037]+
Required: Yes

Response Syntax

```
1 {
2    "[DiscoveredResourceList](#migrationhub-ListDiscoveredResources-response-
         DiscoveredResourceList)": [
3       {
4          "[ConfigurationId](API_DiscoveredResource.md#migrationhub-Type-DiscoveredResource-
              ConfigurationId)": "string",
5          "[Description](API_DiscoveredResource.md#migrationhub-Type-DiscoveredResource-
              Description)": "string"
6       }
7    ],
8    "[NextToken](#migrationhub-ListDiscoveredResources-response-NextToken)": "string"
```

```
9 }
```

Response Elements

If the action is successful, the service sends back an HTTP 200 response.

The following data is returned in JSON format by the service.

** DiscoveredResourceList ** Returned list of discovered resources associated with the given MigrationTask.
Type: Array of DiscoveredResource objects

** NextToken ** If there are more discovered resources than the max result, return the next token to be passed to the next call as a bookmark of where to start from.
Type: String

Errors

AccessDeniedException
You do not have sufficient access to perform this action.
HTTP Status Code: 400

InternalServerError
Exception raised when there is an internal, configuration, or dependency error encountered.
HTTP Status Code: 500

InvalidInputException
Exception raised when the provided input violates a policy constraint or is entered in the wrong format or data type.
HTTP Status Code: 400

ResourceNotFoundException
Exception raised when the request references a resource (ADS configuration, update stream, migration task, etc.) that does not exist in ADS (Application Discovery Service) or in Migration Hub's repository.
HTTP Status Code: 400

ServiceUnavailableException
Exception raised when there is an internal, configuration, or dependency error encountered.
HTTP Status Code: 500

Example

List discovered resources associated with the given MigrationTask

The following example lists the discovered resource name and its description that is associated with the values passed to the required parameters of `MigrationTaskName` and `ProgressUpdateStream` in the request.

Sample Request

```
1 {
2     "ProgressUpdateStream": "SMS",
3     "MigrationTaskName": "sms-12de3cf1a",
4     "NextToken": "",
5     "MaxResults": 1
6 }
```

Sample Response

```
1 {
2     "DiscoveredResourceList": [
3         {
4             "ConfigurationId": "d-server-0025db43a885966c8",
5             "Description": "Amazon Linux AMI release 2016.09"
6         }
7     ]
8 }
```

See Also

For more information about using this API in one of the language-specific AWS SDKs, see the following:

- AWS Command Line Interface
- AWS SDK for .NET
- AWS SDK for C++
- AWS SDK for Go
- AWS SDK for Java
- AWS SDK for JavaScript
- AWS SDK for PHP V3
- AWS SDK for Python
- AWS SDK for Ruby V2

ListMigrationTasks

Lists all, or filtered by resource name, migration tasks associated with the user account making this call. This API has the following traits:

- Can show a summary list of the most recent migration tasks.
- Can show a summary list of migration tasks associated with a given discovered resource.
- Lists migration tasks in a paginated interface.

Request Syntax

```
1 {
2     "[MaxResults](#migrationhub-ListMigrationTasks-request-MaxResults)": number,
3     "[NextToken](#migrationhub-ListMigrationTasks-request-NextToken)": "string",
4     "[ResourceName](#migrationhub-ListMigrationTasks-request-ResourceName)": "string"
5 }
```

Request Parameters

The request accepts the following data in JSON format.

** MaxResults ** Value to specify how many results are returned per page.
Type: Integer
Valid Range: Minimum value of 1. Maximum value of 100.
Required: No

** NextToken ** If a NextToken was returned by a previous call, there are more results available. To retrieve the next page of results, make the call again using the returned token in NextToken.
Type: String
Required: No

** ResourceName ** Filter migration tasks by discovered resource name.
Type: String
Length Constraints: Minimum length of 1. Maximum length of 1600.
Required: No

Response Syntax

```
1 {
2     "[MigrationTaskSummaryList](#migrationhub-ListMigrationTasks-response-
         MigrationTaskSummaryList)": [
3        {
4            "[MigrationTaskName](API_MigrationTaskSummary.md#migrationhub-Type-MigrationTaskSummary
                -MigrationTaskName)": "string",
5            "[ProgressPercent](API_MigrationTaskSummary.md#migrationhub-Type-MigrationTaskSummary-
                ProgressPercent)": number,
6            "[ProgressUpdateStream](API_MigrationTaskSummary.md#migrationhub-Type-
                MigrationTaskSummary-ProgressUpdateStream)": "string",
7            "[Status](API_MigrationTaskSummary.md#migrationhub-Type-MigrationTaskSummary-Status)":
                "string",
8            "[StatusDetail](API_MigrationTaskSummary.md#migrationhub-Type-MigrationTaskSummary-
                StatusDetail)": "string",
```

```
 9      "[UpdateDateTime](API_MigrationTaskSummary.md#migrationhub-Type-MigrationTaskSummary-
            UpdateDateTime)": number
10      }
11    ],
12    "[NextToken](#migrationhub-ListMigrationTasks-response-NextToken)": "string"
13 }
```

Response Elements

If the action is successful, the service sends back an HTTP 200 response.

The following data is returned in JSON format by the service.

** MigrationTaskSummaryList ** Lists the migration task's summary which includes: `MigrationTaskName`, `ProgressPercent`, `ProgressUpdateStream`, `Status`, and the `UpdateDateTime` for each task.
Type: Array of MigrationTaskSummary objects

** NextToken ** If there are more migration tasks than the max result, return the next token to be passed to the next call as a bookmark of where to start from.
Type: String

Errors

AccessDeniedException
You do not have sufficient access to perform this action.
HTTP Status Code: 400

InternalServerError
Exception raised when there is an internal, configuration, or dependency error encountered.
HTTP Status Code: 500

InvalidInputException
Exception raised when the provided input violates a policy constraint or is entered in the wrong format or data type.
HTTP Status Code: 400

PolicyErrorException
Exception raised when there are problems accessing ADS (Application Discovery Service); most likely due to a misconfigured policy or the `migrationhub-discovery` role is missing or not configured correctly.
HTTP Status Code: 400

ResourceNotFoundException
Exception raised when the request references a resource (ADS configuration, update stream, migration task, etc.) that does not exist in ADS (Application Discovery Service) or in Migration Hub's repository.
HTTP Status Code: 400

ServiceUnavailableException
Exception raised when there is an internal, configuration, or dependency error encountered.
HTTP Status Code: 500

Example

List a summary of all the migration tasks

The following example lists a summary of the migration tasks associated with the values passed to the optional parameters of `ResourceName` and `MaxResults`.

Sample Request

```
1  {
2      "MaxResults": 1,
3      "ResourceName": "d-server-0025db43a885966c8"
4  }
```

Sample Response

```
1   {
2       "MigrationTaskSummaryList": [
3           {
4               "Status": "COMPLETED",
5               "ProgressUpdateStream": "SMS",
6               "StatusDetail": "Replication finished",
7               "UpdateDateTime": 1487858882.0,
8               "MigrationTaskName": "sms-12de3cf1a"
9           }
10      ]
11  }
```

See Also

For more information about using this API in one of the language-specific AWS SDKs, see the following:

- AWS Command Line Interface
- AWS SDK for .NET
- AWS SDK for C++
- AWS SDK for Go
- AWS SDK for Java
- AWS SDK for JavaScript
- AWS SDK for PHP V3
- AWS SDK for Python
- AWS SDK for Ruby V2

ListProgressUpdateStreams

Lists progress update streams associated with the user account making this call.

Request Syntax

```
1 {
2    "[MaxResults](#migrationhub-ListProgressUpdateStreams-request-MaxResults)": number,
3    "[NextToken](#migrationhub-ListProgressUpdateStreams-request-NextToken)": "string"
4 }
```

Request Parameters

The request accepts the following data in JSON format.

** MaxResults ** Filter to limit the maximum number of results to list per page.
Type: Integer
Valid Range: Minimum value of 1. Maximum value of 100.
Required: No

** NextToken ** If a `NextToken` was returned by a previous call, there are more results available. To retrieve the next page of results, make the call again using the returned token in `NextToken`.
Type: String
Required: No

Response Syntax

```
1 {
2    "[NextToken](#migrationhub-ListProgressUpdateStreams-response-NextToken)": "string",
3    "[ProgressUpdateStreamSummaryList](#migrationhub-ListProgressUpdateStreams-response-
        ProgressUpdateStreamSummaryList)": [
4       {
5          "[ProgressUpdateStreamName](API_ProgressUpdateStreamSummary.md#migrationhub-Type-
             ProgressUpdateStreamSummary-ProgressUpdateStreamName)": "string"
6       }
7    ]
8 }
```

Response Elements

If the action is successful, the service sends back an HTTP 200 response.

The following data is returned in JSON format by the service.

** NextToken ** If there are more streams created than the max result, return the next token to be passed to the next call as a bookmark of where to start from.
Type: String

** ProgressUpdateStreamSummaryList ** List of progress update streams up to the max number of results passed in the input.
Type: Array of ProgressUpdateStreamSummary objects

Errors

AccessDeniedException

You do not have sufficient access to perform this action.

HTTP Status Code: 400

InternalServerError

Exception raised when there is an internal, configuration, or dependency error encountered.

HTTP Status Code: 500

InvalidInputException

Exception raised when the provided input violates a policy constraint or is entered in the wrong format or data type.

HTTP Status Code: 400

ServiceUnavailableException

Exception raised when there is an internal, configuration, or dependency error encountered.

HTTP Status Code: 500

Example

List progress update streams

The following example lists the progress update streams associated with the account invoking the request and uses the value passed to the optional parameter `MaxResults`.

Sample Request

```
1 {
2     "MaxResults": 2
3 }
```

Sample Response

```
1  {
2      "ProgressUpdateStreamSummaryList": [
3          {
4              "ProgressUpdateStreamName": "DMS"
5          },
6          {
7              "ProgressUpdateStreamName": "SMS"
8          }
9      ],
10     "NextToken": "AYADeDJG11y1VuQBWp87zGdqAkkAXwABABVhd3MtY3J5cHRvLXB1YmxpYy1rZ
11     XkAREFwMOs3MElDWDI4NVJ3RG4vQUVnWFZKa2xNQVI1a2RJZXNNQXZnN2Y4MOpMdjN6Ujhka2VE
12     ZO1RZEFnQ2toUE1Rdz09AAEAB2F3cy1rbXMAS2Fybjphd3M6a21zOnVzLXdlc3QtMjo2MzEzOTQ
13     ONDA2MDg6a2V5L2UzNmUxYTc5LTUyYTUtNDdhZi05YmZjLWUxZDY2MjMyM2EOMwCnAQEBAHieuD
14     SjpG16QpfVPv6L98gI73HcNP7jNyhyIMduHA8a4wAAAH4wfAYJKoZIhvcNAQcGoG8wbQIBADBoB
15     gkqhkiG9w0BBwEwHgYJYIZIAWUDBAEuMBEEDGKeYQzVoDEvBoOEDwIBEIA7KbgCu41sTOBeQaU9
16     BOchDBz6NGrh3AztXyqwJGczR7PiOOJZUPipWyiZDOSwVh/Exbkwm5clUF3VJOkCAAAAAwAABA
17     Ac1MGWKEY/ySGi8kJmVlSZlU6rN/okwmmQCyymv/////8AAAABvAPwOZhHxJ3B4nsQAAAAbahcOb
18     uugm7vytBO5AobE5AWiEJaEEz5kMiYQJtzDfwXM8h9GS8kX7ydocfw0yLCMM9/sLa5JaaqY3yVh
19     K3m9SwqxBS1BBhNhsjPMOZFBVMB12UcG5CW/Qo2rrzpNA/dVrCIweobaBVrxu4X9TkvT7qm67ns
20     IGQM8SHofcfRAGcwZQIwElspH+HhwSxyI59eG6a3juJvgbHBNKwIH72N9Si3TZaTyiskL6QUPH5
```

```
21    Y9PLmtIX7AjEAiZaqz55O+EUmaxiizH76sVuWoCMReEgFJtSm5NM3trucfj2OAiIZ6/MG3bsJ43
22    fZ"
23 }
```

See Also

For more information about using this API in one of the language-specific AWS SDKs, see the following:

- AWS Command Line Interface
- AWS SDK for .NET
- AWS SDK for C++
- AWS SDK for Go
- AWS SDK for Java
- AWS SDK for JavaScript
- AWS SDK for PHP V3
- AWS SDK for Python
- AWS SDK for Ruby V2

NotifyApplicationState

Sets the migration state of an application. For a given application identified by the value passed to `ApplicationId`, its status is set or updated by passing one of three values to `Status`: `NOT_STARTED` | `IN_PROGRESS` | `COMPLETED`.

Request Syntax

```
1 {
2    "[ApplicationId](#migrationhub-NotifyApplicationState-request-ApplicationId)": "string",
3    "[DryRun](#migrationhub-NotifyApplicationState-request-DryRun)": boolean,
4    "[Status](#migrationhub-NotifyApplicationState-request-Status)": "string"
5 }
```

Request Parameters

The request accepts the following data in JSON format.

** ApplicationId ** The configurationId in ADS that uniquely identifies the grouped application.
Type: String
Length Constraints: Minimum length of 1. Maximum length of 1600.
Required: Yes

** DryRun ** Optional boolean flag to indicate whether any effect should take place. Used to test if the caller has permission to make the call.
Type: Boolean
Required: No

** Status ** Status of the application - Not Started, In-Progress, Complete.
Type: String
Valid Values:`NOT_STARTED` | `IN_PROGRESS` | `COMPLETED`
Required: Yes

Response Elements

If the action is successful, the service sends back an HTTP 200 response with an empty HTTP body.

Errors

AccessDeniedException
You do not have sufficient access to perform this action.
HTTP Status Code: 400

DryRunOperation
Exception raised to indicate a successfully authorized action when the `DryRun` flag is set to "true".
HTTP Status Code: 400

InternalServerError
Exception raised when there is an internal, configuration, or dependency error encountered.
HTTP Status Code: 500

InvalidInputException
Exception raised when the provided input violates a policy constraint or is entered in the wrong format or data type.
HTTP Status Code: 400

PolicyErrorException

Exception raised when there are problems accessing ADS (Application Discovery Service); most likely due to a misconfigured policy or the `migrationhub-discovery` role is missing or not configured correctly.
HTTP Status Code: 400

ResourceNotFoundException

Exception raised when the request references a resource (ADS configuration, update stream, migration task, etc.) that does not exist in ADS (Application Discovery Service) or in Migration Hub's repository.
HTTP Status Code: 400

ServiceUnavailableException

Exception raised when there is an internal, configuration, or dependency error encountered.
HTTP Status Code: 500

UnauthorizedOperation

Exception raised to indicate a request was not authorized when the `DryRun` flag is set to "true".
HTTP Status Code: 400

Example

Notify the application state to Migration Hub

The following example communicates the migration status to Migration Hub using the values passed to the required parameters `ApplicationId` and `Status`.

Note
In this example, the `DryRun` parameter is used and set to "true" in order to show the output of the `DryRunOperation` when the user has appropriate permissions to execute the command.

Sample Request

```
1 {
2     "ApplicationId": "d-application-0039038d504694533",
3     "Status": "IN_PROGRESS"
4     "DryRun": true
5 }
```

Sample Response

```
1 An error occurred (DryRunOperation) when calling the NotifyApplicationState operation: Dry Run
     was a success!
2 $
```

See Also

For more information about using this API in one of the language-specific AWS SDKs, see the following:

- AWS Command Line Interface

- AWS SDK for .NET

- AWS SDK for C++

- AWS SDK for Go

- AWS SDK for Java

- AWS SDK for JavaScript
- AWS SDK for PHP V3
- AWS SDK for Python
- AWS SDK for Ruby V2

NotifyMigrationTaskState

Notifies Migration Hub of the current status, progress, or other detail regarding a migration task. This API has the following traits:

- Migration tools will call the `NotifyMigrationTaskState` API to share the latest progress and status.

- `MigrationTaskName` is used for addressing updates to the correct target.

- `ProgressUpdateStream` is used for access control and to provide a namespace for each migration tool.

Request Syntax

```
1  {
2     "[DryRun](#migrationhub-NotifyMigrationTaskState-request-DryRun)": boolean,
3     "[MigrationTaskName](#migrationhub-NotifyMigrationTaskState-request-MigrationTaskName)": "
          string",
4     "[NextUpdateSeconds](#migrationhub-NotifyMigrationTaskState-request-NextUpdateSeconds)":
          number,
5     "[ProgressUpdateStream](#migrationhub-NotifyMigrationTaskState-request-ProgressUpdateStream)
          ": "string",
6     "[Task](#migrationhub-NotifyMigrationTaskState-request-Task)": {
7        "[ProgressPercent](API_Task.md#migrationhub-Type-Task-ProgressPercent)": number,
8        "[Status](API_Task.md#migrationhub-Type-Task-Status)": "string",
9        "[StatusDetail](API_Task.md#migrationhub-Type-Task-StatusDetail)": "string"
10    },
11    "[UpdateDateTime](#migrationhub-NotifyMigrationTaskState-request-UpdateDateTime)": number
12 }
```

Request Parameters

The request accepts the following data in JSON format.

** DryRun ** Optional boolean flag to indicate whether any effect should take place. Used to test if the caller has permission to make the call.
Type: Boolean
Required: No

** MigrationTaskName ** Unique identifier that references the migration task.
Type: String
Length Constraints: Minimum length of 1. Maximum length of 256.
Pattern: [^:|]+
Required: Yes

** NextUpdateSeconds ** Number of seconds after the UpdateDateTime within which the Migration Hub can expect an update. If Migration Hub does not receive an update within the specified interval, then the migration task will be considered stale.
Type: Integer
Valid Range: Minimum value of 0.
Required: Yes

** ProgressUpdateStream ** The name of the ProgressUpdateStream.
Type: String
Length Constraints: Minimum length of 1. Maximum length of 50.
Pattern: [^/:|\000-\037]+
Required: Yes

** Task ** Information about the task's progress and status.
Type: Task object
Required: Yes

** UpdateDateTime ** The timestamp when the task was gathered.
Type: Timestamp
Required: Yes

Response Elements

If the action is successful, the service sends back an HTTP 200 response with an empty HTTP body.

Errors

AccessDeniedException
You do not have sufficient access to perform this action.
HTTP Status Code: 400

DryRunOperation
Exception raised to indicate a successfully authorized action when the DryRun flag is set to "true".
HTTP Status Code: 400

InternalServerError
Exception raised when there is an internal, configuration, or dependency error encountered.
HTTP Status Code: 500

InvalidInputException
Exception raised when the provided input violates a policy constraint or is entered in the wrong format or data type.
HTTP Status Code: 400

ResourceNotFoundException
Exception raised when the request references a resource (ADS configuration, update stream, migration task, etc.) that does not exist in ADS (Application Discovery Service) or in Migration Hub's repository.
HTTP Status Code: 400

ServiceUnavailableException
Exception raised when there is an internal, configuration, or dependency error encountered.
HTTP Status Code: 500

UnauthorizedOperation
Exception raised to indicate a request was not authorized when the DryRun flag is set to "true".
HTTP Status Code: 400

Example

Notify the migration task state to Migration Hub

The following example communicates the latest progress and updates to Migration Hub using the values passed to the required parameters MigrationTaskName and ProgressUpdateStream to tag the correct target and its migration tool. The other parameters in the example are also required to provide details of the task state.

Sample Request

```
1  {
2      "MigrationTaskName": "sms-12de3cf1a",
3      "NextUpdateSeconds": 60,
4      "ProgressUpdateStream": "SMS",
5      "Task": {
6          "ProgressPercent": 77,
7          "Status": "IN_PROGRESS",
8          "StatusDetail": "Migration: Copying image data"
9      },
10     "UpdateDateTime": 1493660853
11 }
```

See Also

For more information about using this API in one of the language-specific AWS SDKs, see the following:

- AWS Command Line Interface
- AWS SDK for .NET
- AWS SDK for C++
- AWS SDK for Go
- AWS SDK for Java
- AWS SDK for JavaScript
- AWS SDK for PHP V3
- AWS SDK for Python
- AWS SDK for Ruby V2

PutResourceAttributes

Provides identifying details of the resource being migrated so that it can be associated in the Application Discovery Service (ADS)'s repository. This association occurs asynchronously after `PutResourceAttributes` returns.

Important

Keep in mind that subsequent calls to PutResourceAttributes will override previously stored attributes. For example, if it is first called with a MAC address, but later, it is desired to *add* an IP address, it will then be required to call it with *both* the IP and MAC addresses to prevent overiding the MAC address. Note the instructions regarding the special use case of the `ResourceAttributeList` parameter when specifying any "VM" related value.

Note

Because this is an asynchronous call, it will always return 200, whether an association occurs or not. To confirm if an association was found based on the provided details, call `ListDiscoveredResources`.

Request Syntax

```
1  {
2      "[DryRun](#migrationhub-PutResourceAttributes-request-DryRun)": boolean,
3      "[MigrationTaskName](#migrationhub-PutResourceAttributes-request-MigrationTaskName)": "string
          ",
4      "[ProgressUpdateStream](#migrationhub-PutResourceAttributes-request-ProgressUpdateStream)": "
          string",
5      "[ResourceAttributeList](#migrationhub-PutResourceAttributes-request-ResourceAttributeList)":
          [
6          {
7              "[Type](API_ResourceAttribute.md#migrationhub-Type-ResourceAttribute-Type)": "string",
8              "[Value](API_ResourceAttribute.md#migrationhub-Type-ResourceAttribute-Value)": "string"
9          }
10     ]
11 }
```

Request Parameters

The request accepts the following data in JSON format.

** DryRun ** Optional boolean flag to indicate whether any effect should take place. Used to test if the caller has permission to make the call.
Type: Boolean
Required: No

** MigrationTaskName ** Unique identifier that references the migration task.
Type: String
Length Constraints: Minimum length of 1. Maximum length of 256.
Pattern: [^:|]+
Required: Yes

** ProgressUpdateStream ** The name of the ProgressUpdateStream.
Type: String
Length Constraints: Minimum length of 1. Maximum length of 50.
Pattern: [^/:|\000-\037]+
Required: Yes

** ResourceAttributeList ** Information about the resource that is being migrated. This data will be used to map the task to a resource in the Application Discovery Service (ADS)'s repository.

Takes the object array of `ResourceAttribute` where the `Type` field is reserved for the following values: `IPV4_ADDRESS` | `IPV6_ADDRESS` | `MAC_ADDRESS` | `FQDN` | `VM_MANAGER_ID` | `VM_MANAGED_OBJECT_REFERENCE` | `VM_NAME` | `VM_PATH` | `BIOS_ID` | `MOTHERBOARD_SERIAL_NUMBER` where the identifying value can be a string up to 256 characters.

- If any "VM" related value is set for a `ResourceAttribute` object, it is required that `VM_MANAGER_ID`, as a minimum, is always set. If `VM_MANAGER_ID` is not set, then all "VM" fields will be discarded and "VM" fields will not be used for matching the migration task to a server in Application Discovery Service (ADS)'s repository. See the Example section below for a use case of specifying "VM" related values.

- If a server you are trying to match has multiple IP or MAC addresses, you should provide as many as you know in separate type/value pairs passed to the `ResourceAttributeList` parameter to maximize the chances of matching. Type: Array of ResourceAttribute objects
Array Members: Minimum number of 1 item. Maximum number of 100 items.
Required: Yes

Response Elements

If the action is successful, the service sends back an HTTP 200 response with an empty HTTP body.

Errors

AccessDeniedException
You do not have sufficient access to perform this action.
HTTP Status Code: 400

DryRunOperation
Exception raised to indicate a successfully authorized action when the `DryRun` flag is set to "true".
HTTP Status Code: 400

InternalServerError
Exception raised when there is an internal, configuration, or dependency error encountered.
HTTP Status Code: 500

InvalidInputException
Exception raised when the provided input violates a policy constraint or is entered in the wrong format or data type.
HTTP Status Code: 400

ResourceNotFoundException
Exception raised when the request references a resource (ADS configuration, update stream, migration task, etc.) that does not exist in ADS (Application Discovery Service) or in Migration Hub's repository.
HTTP Status Code: 400

ServiceUnavailableException
Exception raised when there is an internal, configuration, or dependency error encountered.
HTTP Status Code: 500

UnauthorizedOperation
Exception raised to indicate a request was not authorized when the `DryRun` flag is set to "true".
HTTP Status Code: 400

Example

Put migration resource attributes to associate with resource in repository

The following example sends identifying details of the resource being migrated so that it can be associated with a resource in the Application Discovery Service's repository using the values passed to the required parameters `MigrationTaskName` and `ProgressUpdateStream` to tag the correct target and its migration tool.

The `ResourceAttributeList` parameter is also required to define the resource type and its identifying value. Its `Type` field is reserved for the following values: `IPV4_ADDRESS` | `IPV6_ADDRESS` | `MAC_ADDRESS` | `FQDN` | `VM_MANAGER_ID` | `VM_MANAGED_OBJECT_REFERENCE` | `VM_NAME` | `VM_PATH` | `BIOS_ID` | `MOTHERBOARD_SERIAL_NUMBER` where the identifying value can be a string up to 256 characters.

In this particular example, the user wants to define the resource type by `VM_NAME`, but also has to set the `VM_MANAGER_ID` field as it is always required when setting any other "VM" related fields.

Sample Request

```
{
    "MigrationTaskName":"canary-4c208ae8-9876-5432-1098-b748dd9179d3",
    "ProgressUpdateStream":"canary-017563f9-1234-5678-9de4-cf9d3378d18d",
    "ResourceAttributeList": [
        {
            "Type":"VM_NAME",
            "Value":"v1.1.1.0-cloudfront"
        },
        {
            "Type":"VM_MANAGER_ID",
            "Value":"a7b4c06d-e12f-1234-9gh7-i5j26k1lm2no"
        }
    ]
}
```

See Also

For more information about using this API in one of the language-specific AWS SDKs, see the following:

- AWS Command Line Interface
- AWS SDK for .NET
- AWS SDK for C++
- AWS SDK for Go
- AWS SDK for Java
- AWS SDK for JavaScript
- AWS SDK for PHP V3
- AWS SDK for Python
- AWS SDK for Ruby V2

Data Types

The following data types are supported:

- CreatedArtifact
- DiscoveredResource
- MigrationTask
- MigrationTaskSummary
- ProgressUpdateStreamSummary
- ResourceAttribute
- Task

CreatedArtifact

An ARN of the AWS cloud resource target receiving the migration (e.g., AMI, EC2 instance, RDS instance, etc.).

Contents

Description A description that can be free-form text to record additional detail about the artifact for clarity or for later reference.
Type: String
Length Constraints: Minimum length of 0. Maximum length of 500.
Required: No

Name An ARN that uniquely identifies the result of a migration task.
Type: String
Length Constraints: Minimum length of 1. Maximum length of 1600.
Pattern: `arn:[a-z-]+:[a-z0-9-]+:(?:[a-z0-9-]+|):(?:[0-9]{12}|):.*`
Required: Yes

See Also

For more information about using this API in one of the language-specific AWS SDKs, see the following:

- AWS SDK for C++
- AWS SDK for Go
- AWS SDK for Java
- AWS SDK for Ruby V2

DiscoveredResource

Object representing the on-premises resource being migrated.

Contents

ConfigurationId The configurationId in ADS that uniquely identifies the on-premise resource.
Type: String
Length Constraints: Minimum length of 1.
Required: Yes

Description A description that can be free-form text to record additional detail about the discovered resource for clarity or later reference.
Type: String
Length Constraints: Minimum length of 0. Maximum length of 500.
Required: No

See Also

For more information about using this API in one of the language-specific AWS SDKs, see the following:

- AWS SDK for C++
- AWS SDK for Go
- AWS SDK for Java
- AWS SDK for Ruby V2

MigrationTask

Represents a migration task in a migration tool.

Contents

MigrationTaskName Unique identifier that references the migration task.
Type: String
Length Constraints: Minimum length of 1. Maximum length of 256.
Pattern: [^:|]+
Required: No

ProgressUpdateStream A name that identifies the vendor of the migration tool being used.
Type: String
Length Constraints: Minimum length of 1. Maximum length of 50.
Pattern: [^/:|\000-\037]+
Required: No

ResourceAttributeList

Type: Array of ResourceAttribute objects
Array Members: Minimum number of 0 items. Maximum number of 100 items.
Required: No

Task Task object encapsulating task information.
Type: Task object
Required: No

UpdateDateTime The timestamp when the task was gathered.
Type: Timestamp
Required: No

See Also

For more information about using this API in one of the language-specific AWS SDKs, see the following:

- AWS SDK for C++
- AWS SDK for Go
- AWS SDK for Java
- AWS SDK for Ruby V2

MigrationTaskSummary

MigrationTaskSummary includes `MigrationTaskName`, `ProgressPercent`, `ProgressUpdateStream`, `Status`, and `UpdateDateTime` for each task.

Contents

MigrationTaskName Unique identifier that references the migration task.
Type: String
Length Constraints: Minimum length of 1. Maximum length of 256.
Pattern: `[^:|]+`
Required: No

ProgressPercent

Type: Integer
Valid Range: Minimum value of 0. Maximum value of 100.
Required: No

ProgressUpdateStream An AWS resource used for access control. It should uniquely identify the migration tool as it is used for all updates made by the tool.
Type: String
Length Constraints: Minimum length of 1. Maximum length of 50.
Pattern: `[^/:|\000-\037]+`
Required: No

Status Status of the task.
Type: String
Valid Values:`NOT_STARTED | IN_PROGRESS | FAILED | COMPLETED`
Required: No

StatusDetail Detail information of what is being done within the overall status state.
Type: String
Length Constraints: Minimum length of 0. Maximum length of 500.
Required: No

UpdateDateTime The timestamp when the task was gathered.
Type: Timestamp
Required: No

See Also

For more information about using this API in one of the language-specific AWS SDKs, see the following:

- AWS SDK for C++
- AWS SDK for Go
- AWS SDK for Java
- AWS SDK for Ruby V2

ProgressUpdateStreamSummary

Summary of the AWS resource used for access control that is implicitly linked to your AWS account.

Contents

ProgressUpdateStreamName The name of the ProgressUpdateStream.
Type: String
Length Constraints: Minimum length of 1. Maximum length of 50.
Pattern: [^/:|\000-\037]+
Required: No

See Also

For more information about using this API in one of the language-specific AWS SDKs, see the following:

- AWS SDK for C++
- AWS SDK for Go
- AWS SDK for Java
- AWS SDK for Ruby V2

ResourceAttribute

Attribute associated with a resource.

Note the corresponding format required per type listed below:

IPV4
x.x.x.x
where x is an integer in the range [0,255]

IPV6
y : y : y : y : y : y : y : y
where y is a hexadecimal between 0 and FFFF. [0, FFFF]

MAC_ADDRESS
`^([0-9A-Fa-f]{2}[:-]){5}([0-9A-Fa-f]{2})$`

FQDN
`^[^<>{}\\\\\/?,=\\p{Cntrl}]{1,256}$`

Contents

Type Type of resource.
Type: String
Valid   Values:`IPV4_ADDRESS | IPV6_ADDRESS | MAC_ADDRESS | FQDN | VM_MANAGER_ID | VM_MANAGED_OBJECT_REFERENCE | VM_NAME | VM_PATH | BIOS_ID | MOTHERBOARD_SERIAL_NUMBER | LABEL`
Required: Yes

Value Value of the resource type.
Type: String
Length Constraints: Minimum length of 1. Maximum length of 256.
Required: Yes

See Also

For more information about using this API in one of the language-specific AWS SDKs, see the following:

- AWS SDK for C++
- AWS SDK for Go
- AWS SDK for Java
- AWS SDK for Ruby V2

Task

Task object encapsulating task information.

Contents

ProgressPercent Indication of the percentage completion of the task.
Type: Integer
Valid Range: Minimum value of 0. Maximum value of 100.
Required: No

Status Status of the task - Not Started, In-Progress, Complete.
Type: String
Valid Values:`NOT_STARTED` | `IN_PROGRESS` | `FAILED` | `COMPLETED`
Required: Yes

StatusDetail Details of task status as notified by a migration tool. A tool might use this field to provide clarifying information about the status that is unique to that tool or that explains an error state.
Type: String
Length Constraints: Minimum length of 0. Maximum length of 500.
Required: No

See Also

For more information about using this API in one of the language-specific AWS SDKs, see the following:

- AWS SDK for C++
- AWS SDK for Go
- AWS SDK for Java
- AWS SDK for Ruby V2

Logging AWS Migration Hub API Calls with AWS CloudTrail

Migration Hub is integrated with CloudTrail, a service that captures all of the Migration Hub API calls and delivers the log files to an Amazon S3 bucket that you specify. CloudTrail captures API calls from the Migration Hub console or from your code to the Migration Hub API operations. Using the information collected by CloudTrail, you can determine the request that was made to Migration Hub, the source IP address from which the request was made, who made the request, when it was made, and so on.

To learn more about CloudTrail, including how to configure and enable it, see the AWS CloudTrail User Guide.

Migration Hub Information in CloudTrail

When CloudTrail logging is enabled in your AWS account, API calls made to Migration Hub actions are tracked in CloudTrail log files, where they are written with other AWS service records. CloudTrail determines when to create and write to a new file based on a time period and file size.

All Migration Hub actions are logged by CloudTrail and are documented in the AWS Migration Hub API Reference. For example, calls to the `DescribeApplicationState`, `ImportMigrationTask`, `NotifyApplicationState`, and all of the rest of the Migration Hub actions generate entries in the CloudTrail log files.

Every log entry contains information about who generated the request. The user identity information in the log entry helps you determine the following:

- Whether the request was made with root or IAM user credentials

- Whether the request was made with temporary security credentials for a role or federated user

- Whether the request was made by another AWS service

For more information, see the CloudTrail userIdentity Element.

You can store your log files in your Amazon S3 bucket for as long as you want, but you can also define Amazon S3 lifecycle rules to archive or delete log files automatically. By default, your log files are encrypted with Amazon S3 server-side encryption (SSE).

If you want to be notified upon log file delivery, you can configure CloudTrail to publish Amazon SNS notifications when new log files are delivered. For more information, see Configuring Amazon SNS Notifications for CloudTrail.

You can also aggregate Migration Hub log files from multiple AWS regions and multiple AWS accounts into a single Amazon S3 bucket.

For more information, see Receiving CloudTrail Log Files from Multiple Regions and Receiving CloudTrail Log Files from Multiple Accounts.

Understanding Migration Hub Log File Entries

CloudTrail log files can contain one or more log entries. Each entry lists multiple JSON-formatted events. A log entry represents a single request from any source and includes information about the requested action, the date and time of the action, request parameters, and so on. Log entries are not an ordered stack trace of the public API calls, so they do not appear in any specific order.

The following example shows a CloudTrail log entry that demonstrates the `DescribeApplicationState` action.

```
1  {
2      "eventVersion": "1.05",
3      "userIdentity": {
4          "type": "AssumedRole",
5          "principalId": "AROAIGZQV3RRQMO4RQZCI:sally-90b99f9f-2ffd-4187-9ef1-26b9f22d6419",
```

```
 6        "arn": "arn:aws:sts::123456789012:assumed-role/Sally/sally-90b99f9f-2ffd-4187-9ef1-26
            b9f22d6419",
 7        "accountId": "123456789012",
 8        "accessKeyId": "AKIAIOSFODNN7EXAMPLE",
 9        "sessionContext": {
10            "attributes": {
11                "mfaAuthenticated": "false",
12                "creationDate": "2017-05-23T23:54:04Z"
13            },
14            "sessionIssuer": {
15                "type": "Role",
16                "principalId": "AROAIGZQV3RRQMO4RQZCI",
17                "arn": "arn:aws:iam::123456789012:role/Sally",
18                "accountId": "123456789012",
19                "userName": "Sally"
20            }
21        }
22    },
23    "eventTime": "2017-05-24T00:03:06Z",
24    "eventSource": "migrationhub.amazonaws.com",
25    "eventName": "DescribeApplicationState",
26    "awsRegion": "us-west-2",
27    "sourceIPAddress": "34.223.252.133",
28    "userAgent": "aws-internal/3, sally-generated exec-env/AWS_Lambda_java8",
29    "requestParameters": {"applicationId": "d-application-05d4e9901fa320fa0"},
30    "responseElements": null,
31    "requestID": "5d4eacdc-4014-11e7-925d-65290d4fc127",
32    "eventID": "b12097ee-d121-43f4-a3f8-ca4aa57e6c94",
33    "eventType": "AwsApiCall",
34    "recipientAccountId": "123456789012"
35 }
```

Document History

- User Guide Important Changes
- API Guide Important Changes

User Guide Important Changes

The following table describes important changes to the *AWS Migration Hub* User Guide.

- **API version**: 2017-05-31

- **Latest User Guide documentation update**: March 06, 2018

Change	Description	Date Changed
New guide	This is the first release of the *AWS Migration Hub* User Guide.	August 11, 2017
Discovery walkthrough	Updated to reflect removal of "Deploy agents/connectors" and "Deploy new agents/connectors" from console.	March 06, 2018

API Guide Important Changes

The following table describes important changes to the *AWS Migration Hub* API Guide.

- **API version**: 2017-05-31

- **Latest API Guide documentation update**: March 08, 2018

Change	Description	Date Changed
New guide	This is the first release of the *AWS Migration Hub* API Guide.	August 11, 2017
PutResourceAttributesRequest$ResourceAttributeList	Updated to reflect unused key LABEL removed from Type: Array of ResourceAttribute objects in PutResourceAttributes API.	March 08, 2018